PERSUASION PROFILING

I0044985

'The value of this book transcends professional literature. Kaptein, a digital native for whom the internet appears to have no secrets, clearly explains how the exchange of information on the internet is going to affect our view of the world around us.' – *M&L Managementboek Magazine*

'It's like you're sitting with him at the kitchen table. In clear language, Maurits explains how online marketing will radically change in the future.' – Stefan Wobben, Concept7 Designers

'Indispensable for any marketer who wants to know how to influence the buying and decision making behaviour of potential customers. That would be every good marketer, then.' – Marketingfacts.nl

'A highly entertaining read, requiring little marketing or psychology knowledge. For the educated reader, Kaptein still offers enough new insights and research to make this book the ideal crossover book. Any reader already familiar with Cialdini, *Nudge*, Ariely, Kahneman and others, will welcome this addition to their library.' – Goodreads

'A beginning trend, easily explained and described. This books serves as a first, unique introduction to Persuasion Profiles. It's a handy guide to keep returning to in the coming months and years.' – StanandStacy.com, lead generation specialists

Maurits Kaptein

PERSUASION PROFILING

How the Internet Knows What Makes You Tick

Business Contact Publishers
Amsterdam/Antwerp

© 2015 Maurits Kaptein
Business Contact Publishers
Original title *Digitale verleiding*
Cover design Loudmouth
Interior design Zeno
Author photo Milan Vermeulen

ISBN 978 90 470 0872 9

WWW.BUSINESSCONTACT.NL

TABLE OF CONTENTS

In memory of Professor Clifford I. Nass.

Thank you.

PROLOGUE

Of all the books you could be reading right now, you chose this one. Why did you choose to read this book instead of one of the other books out there? We'd all like to believe that we're reading the book we're currently reading because its content is interesting; after all, you specifically selected this book because it best suits your current wants and needs, and it was the best quality–price trade-off you could find.

Similar reasoning applies to all the other product purchases we've ever made: my current shoes are fantastic value for money, and my car is the best I could afford. But when I think about my T-shirt, I have a minor problem: I'm currently writing this intro-duction as I sit on the couch wearing a Vans T-shirt, and I cannot help but notice that this particular T-shirt (dark blue with white letters that say 'VANS'), purchased for $25 in an outlet near San Jose, is probably not the absolute best value for money. Don't get me wrong: I love this shirt, and I love the brand. But I'm convinced that it should be possible to find the same quality dark blue T-shirt with a number of meaningless white letters for a lower price. These observations sometimes make me doubt my own choices: Why did I end up paying $25, instead of a possible $7, for a fairly plain T-shirt?

WHO AM I?

Before we delve into the product choices I've made, it's only fair to introduce myself briefly. For more than 10 years, I've been study-

ing consumer decision making. Consumer: that's you every time
you buy something. My academic research focuses on the reasons
for specific purchases, and I have meticulously studied the motivations behind seemingly trivial economic choices. In this book, I
focus primarily on the choices made by people who are not clearly
driven by the price–quality trade-off. Basically, I'm interested in
why I bought the VANS T-shirt. However, in recent years, I've become convinced that motivations that go beyond price and quality
affect *all* purchases and many other aspects of human behavior.
Hence, I've conducted research on a variety of economic and lifestyle decisions from a psychological perspective.

At the start of my academic career, I studied economic psychology: the psychology behind economic decisions. I focused primarily on fads, and I wondered why some products that are virtually
useless are suddenly purchased by almost everyone. Perhaps you
remember the Tamagotchi…

After studying fads, I started studying online consumer behavior. Initially, I studied usability, simply put: Where should the
'buy now' product be located so that people can find it easily? And
for the last five years, I've examined the use of psychological sales
techniques in e-commerce.* Through research at the Technical
University of Eindhoven (the Netherlands), as well as at Stanford
University (USA) and the Aalto School of Economics (Finland),
I've tried to understand, and ultimately predict, why people do
or do not buy certain products. I have primarily studied online
purchases because in online commerce, we can directly measure
people's behavior. Using current technologies, we can monitor
consumers continuously and this allows us to structurally study
their behavior. Our recent ability to track people's online activities provides a surprisingly useful research tool for studying consumers' decision-making behavior. The Internet, and specifically

---

* My own research is not limited to the use of sales techniques in e-commerce. I have been studying more broadly how people can be influenced (or
persuaded) by interactive systems. However, this book focuses primarily
on e-commerce not because this is the only interesting human behavior but
because the infrastructure of e-commerce makes studying people's behavior
extremely easy.

online commerce, can be regarded as a telescope or microscope – whichever you feel is more influential in physics – through which human behavior can be studied.

Based on my own research, and that of many others,* it's easy to conclude that consumer behavior is not driven solely by the price–quality trade-off. You might have bought this book just because a colleague recommended it; or perhaps you bought it because it's is a bestseller, indicating that many other people have already bought it. But, then again, perhaps none of these applied: You might have just bought the book because it was on a very special one-day sale. This last argument is probably why I bought my VANS T-shirt.

We like to believe that these 'extra' bits of information (the product is a 'bestseller,' 'special offer,' or 'popular with friends,' etc.) contribute to our informed rational choice. The fact that a product is a bestseller is a sign of quality (why else would so many have bought the product before?), and special discounts change the price–quality trade-off: As the price goes down and the quality remains the same, we're clearly winning.

However, recent psychological research shows that if one randomly adds this kind of information to products, the effects remain the same. If we pitch a book to consumers, asking them how much they are willing to pay for it, and we subsequently pitch the exact same book to another group of similar customers, stating that it is 'almost out of stock,' we find that people in the latter group are willing to pay a higher price.** And, surprisingly, the message does not even have to be true! It seems that we automatically respond to the extra bits of information surrounding the product without necessarily contemplating their effects on the price–quality trade-off.

In this book, I will refer to these 'extra' bits of information, in

---

* For a good introduction, see Cialdini, 2001. Also of interest are the articles by Gretzel and Fesenmaier, 2006 and Eisend, 2008. However, this is only the tip of the iceberg with regard to the social psychological research that shows that our behavior is driven by more than a rational price–quality trade-off.
** An example of this effect can be found in Verhallen and Robben, 1994. I will further detail this study in one of the later chapters.

line with other researchers who have studied purchasing behavior,* as 'persuasion principles'. Some researchers, managers, and marketers have different names for these bits of information; they call them influence principles, sales strategies, persuasive messages, or sales tactics. However, in all cases, we are considering these 'extra' information. Persuasion principles refer to information about a product or service that is not a direct property of the product or service itself. If a product is 'almost out of stock,' which could be caused by poor stock planning on the part of the seller and might have nothing to do with the product itself, this fact still influences our willingness to buy it.

Persuasion principles are not new; they have been studied and used for hundreds of years by good sellers, debaters, and other professional influencers. What is new is the structural use of these principles in online communication to influence and persuade customers while they browse the Internet. This book will detail how this is done.

Selling about 20 years ago

Not so long ago – about twenty years or so – we would go to a physical store every time we wanted to buy something, a few nutty mail-order consumers excluded. After finding and entering the store, it wouldn't be very long before we bumped into the seller – an influencer by nature. We would start talking, and within minutes, the first persuasion principles would enter the conversation. For example, we would be alerted to the fact that our neighbors owned the exact same vacuum cleaner that we were examining and had never experienced any problems. A few minutes later, we would walk out as the happy new owners of a shiny vacuum cleaner, only to find out later that the neighbors didn't even own a vacuum cleaner.

This seller, a great influencer, would be able to persuade a small number of customers per day to make this purchase; they would likely be pretty costly for the consumer electronic store to employ;

---

* For an example of this, see Cialdini and Trost, 1998 and Fogg, 2002. Many more examples exist, but these provide useful introductions.

and not all the customers would appreciate the little sales talk.

Luckily, we have recently entered an era of online shopping. We no longer need to leave the comfort of our homes, we do not need to get wet when it's pouring, and we do not have to talk to sellers. Likewise, the consumer electronics company does not need to employ sellers and can now sell to more people at once. Just to illustrate: A shopkeeper in South Dakota would previously have served his whole town, about 50 families. Today, using the Internet, the same shopkeeper can sell to virtually anyone. We can't deny that selling has changed.

At first, this change sounds good, efficient, and enjoyable for both the customer and the seller. It also sounds almost too good to be true and, in all honesty, is not true. While we currently do sell online, we are actually very bad at selling online. In physical stores, conversion rates – the percentage of customers who enter the store and end up buying something – ranged from almost 100 percent (the supermarket) to about 12 percent (the electronics store). However, the average online merchant would be delighted with a conversion rate of about 5 percent. On average, current online conversion rate runs between 0.5(!) and 2.5 percent.* So while we reach more people, thanks to the advent of e-commerce, we seem to be losing our ability to sell them something. Apparently, we are getting worse at convincing individual customers to make purchases.

WHO SHOULD READ THIS BOOK?

This book describes the things we forgot in our fairly rapid transition from offline to online sales. The book highlights one of the reasons why online conversion rates are surprisingly low compared to offline ones. It also looks at how recent scientific studies, those examining the use of persuasion in particular, can directly contribute to an increase in online conversion if those studies are applied well. This book, at its core, shows how we went from a large

---

* Note that estimated conversion rates differ tremendously between branches, studies, and countries. However, the main point is almost always replicated: Offline conversion is much higher than online conversion.

impact with small reach – the seller was a good influencer but could affect only a limited number of people – to a gigantic reach with only limited impact.

To put the impact back into online marketing this book describes 'persuasion profiles':* profiles that, for each individual customer, describe which psychological persuasion principles are most effective. Persuasion profiles are the next step in increasing the impact of online marketing.

While this book is especially useful if you are trying to sell things online, or intend to in the future, it's even more significant for consumers; which we all are! It is useful to know how persuasion principles are used to influence your behavior. It is valuable to understand why you are specifically offered certain products, news articles, status updates, etc. while your colleagues and friends are offered completely different promotions. With knowledge about the different ways in which you are actively being persuaded while you browse the web, you, as a consumer, can guard against the developments that I describe. Persuasion profiles will impact the future of online marketing, customer relations and multi-channel campaigns – my apologies for the marketing jargon. If you know how these profiles are created, and how their use affects you, you will be able to better protect yourself against unwanted influence.

But let's start where it all began: the physical store...

---

* It is not just online selling that is likely to be affected by the use of persuasion profiles. It is likely that in the near future the application of these profiles will reach far beyond selling. However, we will discuss the possible applications of persuasion profiles in later chapters.

1

WHY THIS BOOK?

'Is this all?' asks the cashier. I say 'yes', put the book The Philosopher and the Wolf *on the counter and grab my credit card. This happened about half an hour after I walked into the bookstore looking for a book for my upcoming trip to a scientific conference in Hawaii.* While purchasing a book may seem trivial, many things happened in that half hour before the book changed owners and it went home in a plastic bag. And we need to understand all these events, all the steps in the sales process, to figure out why conversion rates are much lower online than offline.*

The question 'Why this book?' therefore requires a detailed answer: the idea that this is the 'best' book for the 'best' price is not sufficient. There are so many books; could it ever be possible to make the absolute 'best' choice from among all of them. While I love to make good choices, and might be fairly intelligent, I simply do not have the time for an elaborate analysis of the pros and cons of each book. Luckily, there are lots of other reasons why I had just purchased *The Philosopher and the Wolf.* To understand these, I need to recap the events in the half hour before I got to the checkout counter.

Let's put things in perspective: The day I bought *The Philosopher and the Wolf* was the day before I began my next plane trip.

---

* That weekend I would fly off to Hawaii for a conference called HICSS 2013: The life of an academic can be hard, but surely is not on those days.

The trip would take more than twenty hours, and I was sure that it would be relatively boring, without any form of entertainment. This thought was quite annoying, so I decided I needed a new book. Although I often buy my books online – I generally do not like conversations with physical salespeople – I knew this was not going to happen this time: two books had already got delayed en route from the distribution center to my house, and I really wanted something new before I left.

So, I put on my coat and walk to the bookstore. Now I do have a favorite bookstore, and I know how to get there. However, please note that if I had not been able to find the store, or had no idea of the existence of book stores in general, I would never have made it to the final check-out stage: paying for the actual book.

After entering the store, I walk straight past the novels (these are generally not my taste), the spiritual books (also not quite my taste), and head for the science and philosophy section, way back on the left side of the store.

I know my chances of finding a good book in this section of the store are good, as I already own more than half of the books on display here. I know my way around the shop and do not have to spend time wandering all over the store to find the right section. It is not too large and has a great layout, making it possible to oversee its entire selection. This enables me, and other customers, to quickly get to the selection of books that we want. But obviously, this is not always the case: it does happen that I cannot find something in a store, even though the item is actually in stock.*

So let's recap, up to now I have found the store and located the selection of books that interests me. Next, I have to select the 'best' book from the roughly forty books that remain. Fortunately for me, a helpful sales associate approaches: 'Looking for a gift?' Wearing my T-shirt and sweatpants, I apparently do not appear as

---

*   For me IKEA is a store where this happens frequently. Every time I go there I am unable to find anything I like. However, I often visit friends who seem to buy great stuff there. I just can't find it myself.

a credible buyer of popular scientific or philosophical books. 'No, it's for me,' I answer.

'Then I can recommend this book,' says the sales associate as he picks up *Philosophy for Dummies* from the display table and shows it to me. 'Just this week alone, I have sold four copies of this. It is a real bestseller in this genre and it is an easy read.' I look somewhat concerned and suspicious. First of all I perceive the choice of that book to be an underestimation of my intelligence, but the sales pitch troubles me even more: Do I really look like someone who buys bestsellers?

The seller quickly notices that this choice is not for me and looks around for an alternative. He slowly walks to the leftmost display table: the specials. 'Perhaps this is something for you?' And he points to the book *I Feel, Therefore I Am* by Antonio Damasio. 'Already have it,' I reply. Nevertheless, that is a far better choice by the sales associate. He probably sees my face clearing a bit.

I look around the specials while the sales guy wisely keeps some distance. *The Philosopher and the Wolf* catches my eye. I remember that a year ago this book was recommended to me by a friend, and now it is right here on sale.* Unlike the first attempt by the seller – recommending a bestseller – the recommendation of my friend seems to influence me: I know he often reads books that I can appreciate. Therefore, his recommendations matter to me. And to be honest, I don't mind a bargain.** So, my decision is an easy one.

'Thanks for your help,' I call to the clerk, while I walk over to the checkout desk and place the book on the counter.

THE ONLINE SALES PROCESS
Obviously I have a reason for writing about my recent book purchase in such detail – a book I can recommend by the way. The bookstore I just described has a 'conversion rate' of twenty eight

---

* Thanks Dr. Joris Janssen for recommending the book to me!
** I buy discounted products fairly often. However, I am quite aware that discounted products are often not really cheaper: often sellers increase prices just before offering the product at a 'discount'. In online commerce price fluctuations can be huge. For examples of this see www.camelcamelcamel. com.

percent: more than 1 in 4 people who enter that store leave with a book.* The most successful online bookstores such as the international giant Amazon.com achieve conversion rates of only around 10 percent, if they are lucky. That is not even half the rate of their physical counterparts, and, what is even more striking, is that 10% is the envy of most competitors in other online segments.

My purchasing process for *The Philosopher and the Wolf* would not have differed much online from what took place offline. Online, I also need to first find the actual store. If I know a store, it's simple: I just type in the address in my browser. And if I don't, I go to a search engine and find the store that offers the product (a book) that I want.

This first step is finding the store. This is very important for online sellers, although it is often not included in the conversion figures. After all, if you can't find the store you can't buy anything! Therefore, the first attempts to increase the success of online stores mainly focused on increasing the 'reach' of a store. The current online marketer is known for trying to exploit the new medium to increase the store's reach as much as possible: they focus on higher rankings in search engine results, more links to the shop, and catchy easy-to-remember names,

After finding the online store, step two of the sales process is quite clear as well: the consumer searches product categories or views the recommendations. When I digitally look for a book, I ignore the novels and 'walk' towards 'the corner' of the online store where books about science and philosophy are on display. Much of the attention of web engineers is currently focused on this second step: online stores test their layout to make sure that people can find the categories they are looking for easily. Because many online vendors have a range of stock, many times greater than the offline stores, this step is crucial in online selling.

In addition to offering products in different categories, many smart online stores use formulas and algorithms to actively offer

---

* Here again, estimates of conversion differ greatly. This one is based on a day of counting at my own local bookstore.

specifically targeted products. These 'recommendation systems',[*] for example, keep track of what you were looking for when you entered the shop, for example: 'Novel: Dean Koontz'. Their formulas ensure that you are offered a number of books by Mr. Koontz. And it does not stop there. People who read Dean Koontz also read Stephen King, and hence the store will offer books by that author too. Where the live salesperson tries to select a book for me, mathematical formulas do it online.

Once the selection of products has been reduced to a manageable number, then it's up to me to make my choice, throw the book in my virtual shopping cart, and check out.[**] This is similar to the fourth step of the offline sales process described above.

What we often miss online, however, is step three: the conversation with the sales person. While web technology is already capable of making a selection of products for us, it often ignores an important part of the process; interaction with the seller. Of course, many people would gladly forgo this part, as avoiding real contact with the seller is a popular reason to buy stuff online. Yet, I believe this third step, the active influencing – or 'persuasion' – by the salesperson, partly explains the current conversion gap between online and offline sales. They not only recommend a product – which is what the 'recommendation engines' from Amazon and the like also do – but they use persuasion principles to actively convince me: 'This book is a bestseller' and 'This book is on sale now!' These types of arguments are still often omitted online.

More importantly perhaps, the seller was able to analyze my lack of response to 'This book is a bestseller' and adjusts his persuasion strategy accordingly. This active and dynamic use of psychological persuasion in the sales process is a natural given for

---

[*] Recommender systems, the technology behind these digital recommendations, are a hot topic of research. See for example: Gretzel & Fesenmaier, 2006; Ochi, Rao, Takayama & Nass, 2010; Ricci, Rokach, Shapira & Kantor, 2011. In Chapter 4 I will describe 'recommender systems' in more detail.
[**] The check-out process in online shopping has proved non-trivial. Many customers fail to buy products that they put in their shopping carts. This is a very active area of user studies: how do we make sure the check-out process is simple enough?

good sellers, but is for the most part lacking online. We just seem to miss out step three.*

Recently, there have been definite signs of step three emerging online: you do encounter 'special' and 'bestseller' offers. And increasingly, websites show how often a product is purchased, if it is a bestseller, and how many are still left. These persuasion strategies are already increasing the conversion rates of many online sellers. This is starting to bridge the gap between online and offline selling. But still these websites are nowhere near as effective as real life salespeople. Good salespeople keep track of the conversation: they remember which persuasive argument works for you and which do not. The seller doesn't just select a product for you; they also carefully select the right argument to successfully sell that product. The salesperson learns and adapts by observing your behavior. In doing this, the salesperson implicitly creates a profile, not only about the type of product you want, but also about how this product should be pitched to you. And, in part, it is this profile that makes an offline salesperson more effective than our online sellers.

SEARCHING FOR IMPACT
In an online store you are not assisted by a real-life salesperson who can gradually adjust their strategy during the conversation. Nevertheless, the way you are persuaded can essentially be the same. In this book I will show you how, on the basis of the studies and experiments that I carried out with Dr. Dean Eckles and many others, the natural, age-old sales process can be carried out online. You will see how in the course of time we have evolved from a small 'reach' with high 'impact' (and by the latter I mean: the influence that the seller has on a single person) to a huge reach with hardly any significant impact. This transition began centuries ago with the introduction of the printing press. Much later, marketing campaigns in mass media channels dramatically

---

* An aspect that is often overlooked in step three is the power of reciprocity: the salesman helps us find the products, so we feel inclined to return the favor by buying a product. See for more information about reciprocity: Komorita, Hilty & Parks, 1991.

increased the range of physical stores: many vendors could now potentially reach out to millions of customers. The advent of the Internet has ultimately led to a situation in which anyone with an Internet connection can sell products to virtually everyone else in the world. The reach therefore is enormous, but the impact of each individual sales attempt is often minimal.

The first thing that online retailers tried to do was increase their reach by ensuring that their stores could be found (discussed in detail in Chapter 3), which even today is still a major concern. And that's not without reason: being easily discoverable by the right customers increases not only the reach of online stores, but also their impact: they ensure they attract the right audience.

The next step was that online sellers started to focus on making sure that the customer could find the right products (Chapter 4). This is accomplished by the use of so-called 'recommendation systems', that use mathematical algorithms to select the right products for the right customer. You might wonder how these recommendation systems work, and what they know about you. What kind of profile do they create and what information do they need to do so? Chapter 4 will give you a peek behind the scenes of the current 'intelligence' of computers.*

Even though these steps have improved the impact of online selling over the past fifteen years, online sales systems are still performing a lot worse than the offline salesperson. This is where our psychology comes into play: we will study not only how the brain works (Chapter 5), but also the psychological principles that persuade people (Chapter 6). There is a lot to gain for online sellers, because the developments in online marketing have, so far, not paid enough attention to the consumers' decision-making processes. There is actually a lot known in psychology and marketing about this subject even though the knowledge is only sparsely put to use online. Despite the fact that the difference between offline and online impact, to a large extent, can be explained by the ab-

---

* Of course there are many books on 'how to be found' (called Search Engine Optimalisation (SEO)) and on 'recommender systems'. I will give a brief introduction in this book, but for more information see Ricci et al., 2011.

sence of active and interactive psychological influence, focusing on the use of persuasion in online selling will change the future of marketing.*

After reviewing the key insights from psychology, our journey takes us through uncharted territory. How can we best apply our knowledge of psychological persuasion? First we will carry out some experiments that demonstrate that a single, well-chosen persuasion principle is often more effective than using a multiple of principles simultaneously (Chapter 7). Next, we will discover that individuals respond differently to psychological persuasion (Chapter 8) and that they are consistent in their responses; meaning that if you can be persuaded to buy shoes using one method, then you can be convinced to buy a new phone in the same way.

Then we will arrive at the 'missing link', step three in the sales process: persuasion profiles. What real-life salespeople do, online sales systems can also do now, thanks to persuasion profiling. You will discover new research into online selling, first to prove that our theory of persuasion profiles actually works (Chapter 9), and later to find out how we can create a profile that describes which persuasion principles you are the most susceptible to (Chapter 10). This profile is dynamically adjusted based on your responses to persuasion attempts from multiple online stores. The profile is then used to select the most appropriate persuasion strategy.

Persuasion Profiles are the 'marketing currency' of the future. They change your online shopping experience and follow you in applications that reach far beyond the web. Not only will you be persuaded while making a product purchase or even trying to lose weight using a mobile application that tracks your activity patterns, but similar profiles will likely be used to persuade you to make a choice for a political party as well, More and more applications will use technology to – consciously or unconsciously – influence your behavior using 'persuasion'.

We will end this journey with a discussion of the implications

---

of persuasion profiles for your privacy and autonomy: The use of persuasion profiles does raise ethical questions after all.

How ONLINE PERSUASION WORKS

From the bricks and mortar store owner that learns that you like to buy what the neighbors also bought, or rather what they could not afford, this book guides you to the use of persuasion profiles: Individual profiles that online stores can use to create the same impact as the bricks and mortar store owner. Persuasion profiles based on your personal reaction to persuasion strategies are still fairly new, but certainly not transient. The technology is ready. We can measure how you react and we can calculate what strategy works best for you personally. And you, you're ready too, though maybe you have not realized it yet. Your response to your bricks and mortar sales clerk in reality will be no different from your reaction to this new technology.

However, it does feel different when a website or an online store maintains your profile compared to your local shop owner. Despite the fact that persuasion is everywhere – people influence each other, the newspaper affects your opinions, and television ads try to persuade you to buy something – many people with whom I speak at conferences find this new technology unethical or downright scary.

Persuasion profiles are scary. Indeed, there are some major differences between the profiles online and the store owners who know how to sell you something in person. The persuasion technology is theoretically able to follow you, not just in a single store, but across all stores that you visit online. And it does not stop at the online store: your reactions to psychologically based persuasion can be recorded when you use social media, when you use an online voting guide, or even when you seek help from an online psychologist. The technology has the ability to track you in places where the store owner cannot.*

---

* By now the tracking of consumers is starting to be regulated. In Europe regulations are pretty strict: online marketers are no longer allowed to follow everyone everywhere. However, the exact compliance with these new regulations remains to be seen.

Moreover, the technology can remember and store much more information about you than any bricks and mortar store owner can. Because you return every week, and that neighbor trick apparently works time after time, the salesperson easily remembers it. But when you have been away for a couple of weeks on vacation that knowledge easily fades away. With digitally-stored persuasion profiles, things are quite different. The profile can be stored permanently. All information about all your reactions to persuasion principles can be stored, used and perhaps even sold to third parties. These two properties, their use in multiple situations and the almost infinite availability of information, make persuasion profiles scary.

But we have not reached that point yet: technology can measure or remember anything and everything, but it's still rather stupid. While the seller in the bookstore immediately recognized that I was really not impressed by the bestseller approach, an online seller can not just 'see' this. The online store has to learn these facts based on your mouse clicks and your purchasing behavior. It will therefore be some time before the technology has reached a point where it has the same impact as sellers in the real world. Fortunately for you, the consumer, you are here at the right time to witness this. And if you are an online seller you will, by reading this book, be one of the front-runners in persuasion profiling.

SUMMARIZING

Salespeople have more impact than online stores because they use personalized psychologically based persuasion strategies. Online stores, and other technologies that try to influence us, can also increase their impact by using persuasion. This book explains how. On the one hand it outlines how you can use persuasion to influence people's behavior. On the other hand it also explains how you, as a consumer, can defend yourself against such tactics.

Each chapter focuses on a different aspect for increasing the impact. At the end of each chapter I will summarize the main points so that you can scan through the summaries and decide which are the most interesting for you. What follows is a brief summary of the 'sneak preview' this chapter provided about the contents of this book:

- Economic decisions are not just based on rational decisions
- Psychological persuasion principles play a large role in the human decision-making process.
- In order to sell anything a store first has to be findable.
- Secondly, the customer has to be able to find the product in the store's stock
- Salespeople can use psychological persuasion principles to increase the chances of a sale.
- Just like a good salesperson remembers which persuasion tactics worked for a particular customer, online stores can learn this too. In which case the online store uses a persuasion tactic.
- Persuasion profiles bear many similarities with good salespeople. But they are bit scary too: They can be used in more than one store at the same time, retain endless data and be kept indefinitely.

More than 95 percent of people that read this first chapter have finished reading this whole book with great pleasure.*

---

* There you go, a bit of psychological persuasion. Just so you can get used to the idea.

2

REACHING MORE AND MORE PEOPLE

'Yes, this is a great book!' remarks the bookseller while he scans the price of my book. The seller from the previous chapter has followed me to the cash register, as I apparently have to check the book out with him. He carefully places the book, The Philosopher and the Wolf, *on the counter.*

'We have a few more books like this on offer. What would you think of Justice *by Michael Sandel? Normally it would cost you $15, but you can get it for $10 today.'*

… (I ponder) …

'Allright, add that one as well…'

While initially I only needed a book for my flight to Hawaii, I now end up with two books. While walking out I start to analyze my purchases. I really didn't need two books; the two that I ordered online are on their way and I am sure they will have arrived by the time I return from Hawaii. What is more, it was never my intention to buy more than one book. A short book for the trip to Hawaii, that was all. The bookseller obviously thought differently…

During our short time together, the bookseller has apparently been able to learn some things about me and use them to influence me. First of all, the seller has seen what kinds of products I like: books about philosophy, but not for dummies. Then, he has noticed that I'm not necessarily looking for a bestseller. The fact that many people have already bought the book doesn't seem to matter much to me. But when I saw a special offer I was quickly sold.

While checking out, the seller made full use of his insights: he sought out the right product – another philosophy book – and used the correct persuasion principle, the discounted price offer. The seller found the correct item and offered it to me in the right way. Because of this combination of product knowledge and mode of delivery, the seller was able to persuade me into an unplanned purchase.*

USING PERSUASION TO CREATE IMPACT

'Impact', in the remainder of this book, will be defined as the ability to influence the consumer during an individual sales moment. This is obviously an over-simplification, since impact will often likely depend on previous contact, and contacts with others too. But it is not overly simplistic: this definition of impact is very useful in illustrating the differences between sales in the physical store and sales in the current online stores.

Let's take a closer look at impact and place it in its historical context. We start at a time – several centuries ago – where virtually all forms of influencing decision processes took place in person, just like my own interaction in the bookstore.

In those times the impact that a persuader – the seller – had on their 'target' – yes, someone just like you – was very high, assuming he was a good salesman. Because each interaction was personal, a good influencer could adapt to his target, readjust, and apply a variety of possible psychological strategies (although many of them had not yet been formally described at that time; that would not happen until many years later) thereby exerting a lot of influence. So the traditional seller had a lot of impact.

This impact from person to person, the ability to influence others, was deemed an important quality even in ancient times. The ancient Greeks esteemed Peitho, the god of persuasion. He is per-

---

* In this particular case I was ultimately very happy with the purchase. But this is not always the case. (See the discussion in Chapter 11).

haps not as well-known as Aphrodite and Apollo, but his existence in Greek writings indicates that the Greeks valued person-to-person impact. In addition, we know of Aristotle's argumentation theory. It is still used and taught today, teaching you how you can influence people. Aristotle's concepts of 'logos', 'ethos' and 'pathos' are also known as the three ways to influence people; through logic, through credibility of authority, or by the use of emotion. The ancient Greeks were already busy increasing impact.

REACHING THE MASSES

Given that the impact of communication between two people can be very significant, and for centuries people have been engaged in describing, explaining, and increasing that impact, there remains a limit to the range of human-to-human communication. Even Aristotle, over his whole lifetime, could only talk to a limited number of people. His impact on each individual with whom he spoke may well have been astounding, but the range of his impact at that time probably left something to be desired.

After the era of pure human-to-human communication, other forms of communication appeared. Mediated communication increased the range of people affected: a single person was able to reach out to multiple people at once. Figure 1 illustrates the human-to-human impact we know from ancient times, and it further shows how the range of our communication evolved over time: how many 'targets' an individual influencer could reach in different times.

Before the advent of things like the printing press, radio and television, the reach of people was quite small. Aristotle could talk to only a few people, and his writings were available to only a handful of students. In principle however, his books could be read by more people than the writer could personally appeal to thus extending his range. In Aristotle's time books were still scarce, but the printing of books became cheaper over time. After the invention of the printing press in 1440, an author could reach thousands, if not hundreds of thousands of people. Through radio (± 1890) and television (± 1920) the range of potential influencers further increased. Today we are at a point where an influencer

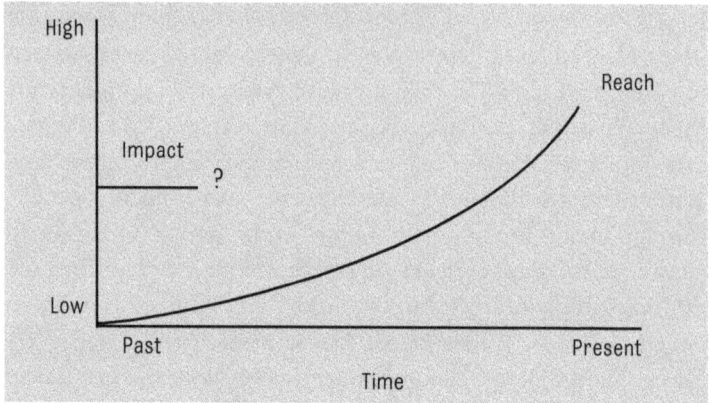

Figure 1: An overview of reach and impact over the years. It is clear that reach has increased tremendously: technology has allowed us to reach more and more people. Impact starts high: a good salesperson can really influence individuals. In order to keep a bit of the suspense, I have not yet extended the line for impact. I'll do so in figure 2.

– and that can be anyone – has the potential to reach the entire world.

At first people were shocked by the dramatic increase in the range of communication. At the time of mass media's ascent, the power of the mass media was frequently described and criticized by communications experts.* Researchers mostly focused on the devastating effects: mass media with such a huge range would spoil our children and our societies. We, the people, would be transformed into an inert mass that obeyed the many attempts of mass media raining down on us. These initial doomsday scenarios about the impact of mass media have not completely come true.

Recently, we have added the Internet to our mediated communication options, which has greatly increased the available options for those trying to influence others. Television and radio

* Several theorists have studied the effects of mass media and how they would destroy our society. There are a number of good introductions. For example see: Baran, 2005.

were available to only a select number of influencers. Today, anyone, anywhere, can potentially reach the entire world population. Finally, the presence of media in our lives has also changed over time: where we spent a few hours a week in front of our television in the past, most of us can now be reached at any time: by our smartphones and computers we are always connected.

Using the Internet we cannot just reach a huge number of people; we can address these people personally too. An influencer can show you a different message than the one he shows your neighbor. You can imagine that this development led to further discussions by communication scholars: Numerous scholars have warned how our world will perish because of the huge reach of the Internet. There are already several theories about internet-based influencing and its disastrous consequences. Writer Eli Pariser, echoing scientist Dean Eckles, mentions the 'Friendly World Syndrome': because we see only filtered information on the Internet and actually see only what we like. This changes our worldview. We think the world is more like us than it actually is. The consequence of this would then be that we become less tolerant of dissent, and end up getting more polarized and fragmented.[*]

INFLUENCING MORE AND MORE PEOPLE

How does the initial impact of human-to-human communication compare to the increased range? In Figure 2, the dream of every marketer and the nightmare of communication scholars is shown: we reach more people, and we maintain impact, so our overall effect grows. As the range increases and the impact remains constant, the effect grows and the inert masses are sent in every feasible direction.

The ultimate effect of an influencer – the dotted line in Figure 2 – could be formalized as a function of the impact of each attempt to influence, and the number of attempts that one makes – the range. So:

$$E = B \times I$$

---

[*] An interview with Dean Eckles can be found in the bestseller *The Filter Bubble*. See Pariser, 2011.

The effect, E, is equal to the range, R, multiplied by the impact, I.* This simple formula basically says that if you can reach and convince more people then the effect of your message is huge. Both reach and impact directly contribute to the effect. As long as the impact remains the same, as shown in figure 2, and the range increases exponentially, the effect will ultimately skyrocket.

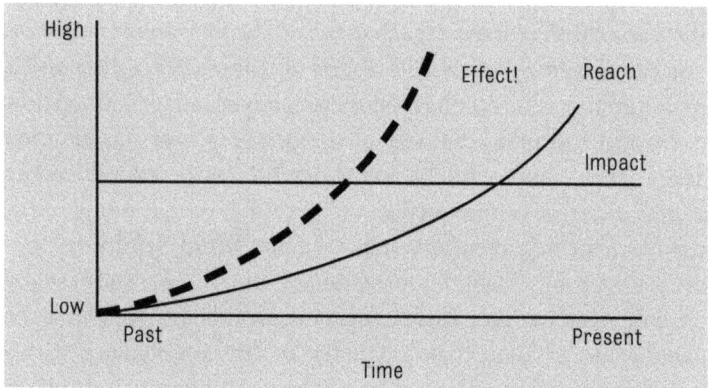

Figure 2: Another graph showcasing impact and reach over the years. This time I have extended the impact according to the marketers' dreams: it remains constant. The total effect is drawn too. Effect is a function of impact and reach. Due to the growing reach and the constant impact, the final effect explodes. Again, this is the dream scenario.

A DREAM COME TRUE

Let's take a better look at the idea that impact and reach together determine the effect of a message. We start by making a couple of estimates.

Suppose you were a salesperson before 1450 – about the time that book printing really began to take off. You were a good seller, and thus a good influencer. If you were asked about your impact,

---

* From now on I will try to avoid formulas. This is one of the few in the book. Please don't be discouraged.

you would give yourself a 10: almost every customer who walked through the door bought something, and often the customer would even buy things that he at first did not think he really needed. However, the number of people walking into your store was limited – most people in the city came to visit you, but the city was not very large. Unlike your impact, your reach was not very large. For argument's sake, let's say that your impact was indeed as high as you own assessment, a 10, but the range was fairly small: say a 1.*

Table 1 illustrates this simple idea in a bit more detail. The left-hand column shows the time – we go through the years as you read further down. The second column shows your assessment of the impact, and the third column shows your range. The last column shows the final effect that you had before 1450: 10 × 1 = 10. That made for a fine living as a salesman at that time.

In 1460 your first advertising brochure came out, you were quick to see the benefits. Now not only the people in your city, but also in surrounding cities, could read about your store and your product. Your range expanded significantly, and you expected your effect to increase too. The estimated effect that you now might have was quite a bit higher, 10 × 10 = 100. Your impact remained constant at 10, equal to the time before the publication of your brochure, but your range increased. Because of this increased range, the final effect increased.

And we'll continue with the same idea, conveniently assuming that you grew to be quite old; of course is realistically impossible but this is just conceptual so bear with me. After the printing press, radio and television were soon to follow, and since you are a powerful and effective seller, you had access to these media as well. Your impact is still 10, but your new range is 100, and thus you again increase your effect according to the formula: your latest effect is 10 × 100 = 1000! And so on!

---

* '10 what?' You might ask yourself. For this example I will not define a measure of effect. I hope you don't mind. I am just putting up some numbers to explain how impact and reach might relate.

Time	Impact	Reach	Effect
Before 1450	10	1	10
Printing press	10	10	100
Radio, TV	10	100	1000
Internet	10	1000	10000

Table 1: The hypothetical development of impact, reach and effect throughout the years. As a supplement to the illustrations in this chapter, in case you are more numerically than visually inclined.

In the last twenty years, with the advent of the Internet and the ability to reach consumers through their computers, phones or tablets, your reach has grown even further, and your effectiveness is now off the charts – see Figure 2. Your effect is 10 × 1000 = 10000! With those kinds of effects, the communication theorists might be proven right. This is scary.

The accumulation of effect as described above is what marketers wished to achieve. And, at the same time, it is exactly what communication experts feared. In this scenario, everyone with some basic influencing skills, and therefore the means to achieve impact, could reach a great number of people and therefore have a very great effect. We, the people, then truly become an inert mass, at the mercy of the influencer's whims.

REALITY PROVES MORE PROBLEMATIC

If we take a look around us now, we notice that today's youth is not completely ruined, and that society has not yet fallen apart. The first doomsayers among communication scientists seem to be proven wrong. This doesn't mean the marketers got it right either. While they see that they are reaching more and more people, this is not having the effect they wanted. The traditional bookstore attracted hundreds of people on a given day and had an impact of 25 percent. For argument's sake: the store had an effect of 25 books sold per day. Today the online bookstore reaches 10000 people per day. Therefore, the dream of the marketer is focused on maintaining an impact of 25 percent, and ultimately an effect of 2500 books sold per day.

But, as we saw in Chapter 1, this is not reality: human-to-human sales may well have an impact of 25 percent, but this is not the case for computer-to-person sales. Online the estimates range from 1 to 5 percent. Rather than 2500 books per day, in the worst case only 250 books per day are sold. Increased competition aside, we are still achieving sales increases because of the Internet. Disappointingly, this reality-based estimate is still pretty far from the marketer's dream. They are overestimating the real effect – like the communication experts before them.

Let's look at a more realistic graph (Figure 3) showing the relationship between reach and impact and the associated Table. Table 2 starts out in the same way as the dream scenario in Table 1: Impact 10, range 1 and 10 as the effect. But as the reach grows over time, the impact – this time the impact labeled 'real impact' tapers off.

While the reach is growing, the ultimate effect is growing much more slowly than initially expected. In reality, the effect is therefore better described by a formula that looks like this:

$$E = (I - \alpha B) \times B$$

In this new formula the final effect still depends on the reach R and impact I. However, the real impact, $I - aR$, decreases as the reach grows This suggests that as you reach more people, you will have less impact per interaction. The final effect is not just the product of reach R and impact I: the real impact is declining as the reach grows.

Time	Real impact	Reach	Effect
	(I – B)	B	E
Before 1450	10	1	10
Printing press	1.1	10	11
Radio, TV	.12	100	12
Internet	.013	1000	13

Table 2: The real trend for impact and reach over the years. Because impact decreases with increases in range, the effect is less than expected. See Figure 3.

To truly understand this, we need to really understand the significance of α in formula 2. This α in fact indicates how the real impact decreases as the reach grows. If α were zero, then the formula would be exactly the same as formula 1. However, if α is greater than zero – which appears to be the case – then each time the reach grows the impact is reduced. Table 2 shows some hypothetical numbers to help illustrate my case more clearly, but on the basis of the differences in conversion between the online bookstore and the physical store, we can estimate the true α at this moment, and represent the decrease in impact as the reach increases. Theoretically, we can then quantify the lost impact as a function of the increased reach.

The situation depicted in the following Figure 3 is, therefore, closer to the real situation in which we find ourselves. The ultimate effect as a function of the reach and impact does not grow as fast as we expected: the effect is only marginally increasing.

WHY DO WE LOSE IMPACT?

Why do we need as a factor in the effect computation? In other words, why does the true impact lessen with the increase in reach? Various researchers have devoted their time to this topic. One can deduce three plausible reasons for the reduction of impact as reach grows. I will address them one by one.

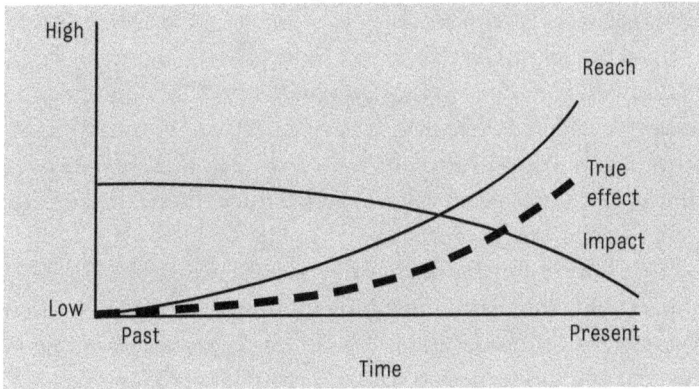

Figure 3: The last, and most accurate, graph depicting the interplay between impact and reach on effect. The reach increases over the years, but the impact of each individual contact lessens. As a result, the true effect is far below the expectations of the dream scenario.

First of all, impact may decrease due to the fact that a different type of customer is being selected because of the increased reach. In the past, almost everyone who came to a bricks and mortar store consciously went there with the sole purpose of buying a product. Now that the reach has increased the store might also attract people who just stray in with little or no intention of buying. That alone is likely to lead to a reduction in impact.

Second, even if the people you reach are interested, they can be turned off easily: the people you reach might be overwhelmed by the increased supply that many online vendors offer. Supply is known to grow in parallel with reach thus increasing the choices for customers. This choice does not always make life easier and often leads to slower or delayed decisions. More choice – paradoxically – often leads to a reduction in impact.

That seems crazy, since more choice should mean there is something for everybody, and so one would expect the impact to rise. But that is not the case, as was demonstrated convincingly in the field of social psychology by the works of Barry Schwartz and Andrew Ward. In 2003, these two researchers carried out a simple but ingenious experiment. They were interested in selling jam in a large US supermarket To research the sales of jam, they placed a table with jams close to the check-out lanes. On some days, the researchers offered more than twenty-four flavors of jam, while on other days only six. The results were very clear: If there were *more* choices, *fewer* jars of jam were sold! This study showed that greater choice lead to a reduced impact. *

The third and by far the most important reason for the loss of impact lies in the change from human-to-human communication to mediated communication: if you find the store, are willing to buy and you experience no stress due to an abundance of choice, you still can't find a real salesperson in the online store. There is product description, there are pictures of products, and perhaps there is even a short video. But it is different. It feels different. The interaction between you and the seller does not exist.

The shift from human-to-human communication as it took place in a physical store, to book-to-human communication, television-to-human communication, or computer-to-human communication is often cited as the main reason for the loss of impact. People simply respond differently to media – books, radio, television, and computers – than to real people. We seem to lose impact when we communicate through a medium rather than directly.

COMPUTERS ARE NOT THE SAME AS HUMANS

By increasing the reach and communicating through a medium, something definitely seems to have changed. Many researchers, therefore, are of the opinion that online sellers are bound to lose a certain amount of impact. Computers cannot, as these researchers argue, use persuasion in the way humans can. And it is precisely these kinds of psychological mechanisms that distinguish the good influencer, the one with a high impact, from the bad. If mediated communication cannot utilize these psychological princi-

---

* Barry Schwartz dedicated a number of publications to the *'paradox of choice'*. An overview of his work, including a description of the 'jam' study, can be found in: Schwartz, 2003.

ples, then it is bound to suffer a low impact. Computers and other media are by definition bad influencers.

'Psychological and social persuasion effects exhibit themselves between humans, and not between human and computer. As the reach grows, impact is reduced.' Well, that sounds plausible.

OR ARE THEY?

Rather than blindly accepting the idea that people react differently to computers than to other people, Professors Reeves and Nass at Stanford University decided to check if that really was true in a study conducted in the eighties. Do people really respond so differently to computers than to other people, and will we always lose impact if we use media to increase our reach?

First Reeves and Nass decided to research a number of well known psychological effects. Together with their student BJ Fogg[*] they reviewed a very strong effect in human-to-human interaction: the effect of compliments.

It has long been known in psychology that compliments ('That was a great presentation, very nice to hear') have a positive effect on the image that people have of other people. If I pay you – one of the smartest and most attractive readers of this book – a compliment, you will probably not only find me friendlier but also more intelligent. Moreover, you will probably predict that I make fewer mistakes in my work.[**]

These well-known psychological studies of human-to-human compliments, however, showed that not only are the effects of compliments very great, but also that unsubstantiated, or rather untruthful, compliments largely have the same effect. This type of insincere 'flattery' has almost the same effect as a real compli-

---

[*] During the course of this research, BJ Fogg was a student under professor Nass. He is currently a professor at Stanford, and the founder of the Persuasive Technology Lab. With his book *Persuasive Technology: Using Computers to Change What We Think and Do*, BJ Fogg is one of the most influential people in this area. Fogg, 2002 also Fogg & Eckles, 2007.
[**] Social scientists have carried out a great deal of research into the effects of flattery and always arrived at the same positive results. For flattery by computers, see Fogg & Nass, 1997, or Johnson, Gardner & Wiles, 2004.

ment: you feel the giver of the compliment is friendlier, smarter, and more capable.

To test this same principle in computer-to-human communication, Professor Nass came up with a little task that a person had to perform together with a computer. When a test subject arrived at the laboratory, they were asked to take their place behind a computer. Then the subject was instructed to play the well-known game of 'twenty questions': One of the players mentally focuses on an animal, and the other player must guess the right animal through twenty yes and no questions. In this case, the computer asked the questions, and the participant said 'yes' or 'no'.

If, after twenty questions the computer could not guess the animal – which was actually always the case – the computer asked the participant to type in a good follow-up question. The subject was told that by making a good suggestion, the computer could then learn how to play the game better. After the subject had typed his suggestion, he received a response from the computer: half the participants got no significant feedback, while the computer indicated to the other half that they had done 'very well'. This distinction was made to test the effect of compliments from computers to humans.

The participants were then asked whether they wanted to evaluate the computer: were the questions that they had received from the computer good ones? Was the final answer correct? While everyone had been given the same questions, at the end of the experiment people who had received the computer's compliments found that the computer was smarter, and that the computer more often asked a good question. This experiment showed conclusively that compliments from computers to humans also have an effect. This study made a first dent in the assumption that communication from computer to human is materially different from communication between humans.

Even more surprising was the finding in a third group of people. These participants also received compliments for the follow up questions they suggested, but they had been told before the experiment that those had nothing to do with their performance and were randomly generated. They were advised to ignore them.

To the researchers' surprise, they found that even in the case of obvious flattery, people were more positive about the computer. So it appears flattery can even work between computers and humans!

HUMAN REACTIONS TO COMPUTERS

After this initial research Professors Reeves and Nass developed a theory which they labeled the 'media equation'*: 'people react in the same way to interactive media as they react to other people'. To further substantiate their theory, they looked into other psychological and social effects in human-to-computer interaction that normally occur only between people.

It has been known for some time that people tend to evaluate others more positively when they are providing the feedback personally, rather than providing it to a third party. When you evaluate the performance of one of your colleagues, you are likely to be a lot more positive face-to-face than when you are talking to another colleague or your boss about them.**Accordingly, they looked at the impact of computer-to-human interaction for evaluating the performance of computers.

Again they asked some people if they wanted to perform a task together with a computer. This time around, the participants in the study were asked to solve a puzzle. The computer behind which the participants sat, helped them to solve the puzzle by giving suggestions.

After solving the puzzle, the participants were asked to evaluate the computer's suggestions. Reeves and Nass again found, to their surprise, that the participants who completed the evaluation form on the computer that they had previously used to solve the puzzle 'together' were more positive than participants who filled out the form on a different computer. This experiment showed that people are more positive when it comes to the person itself – a computer

---

* The research by Reeves and Nass, with a number of other surprising results, is covered in Reeves & Nass, 1996.
** Humans already have a tendency to be more positive in direct evaluations. The tendency to suppress negative evaluations is also known as the 'MUM' effect. See Rosen & Tesser, 1970. The acronym MUM stands for: 'To keep Mum about Undesirable Messages'.

this time – than when they interact with another person (computer).*

The most striking finding in the whole series of studies that Reeves and Nass carried out into the interactions between humans and computers is their replication – the beautiful scientific term for imitation.

As early as 1971 Professor Henri Tajfel showed, through the so called 'group polarization' experiments, the shocking effects of group membership.** Group polarization is the phenomenon whereby people who are members of one group separate themselves from other groups. In the first human-to-human experiments, young visitors to a summer camp were divided into two groups: one group with red T-shirts and one with blue T-shirts. For the record, these were children who did not know each other, were collectively dropped off at summer camp by their parents and then randomly given a differently colored T-shirt. Besides the T-shirt, there was nothing to bind the children to their group or stop them from bonding with the other group.

However, Professor Tajfel demonstrated that within a very short time a close relationship developed between the members of the same colored group, especially when the two groups performed competitive tasks,. At the same time, a strong aversion to members of the other group developed very quickly. Children with a red T-shirt soon found other children with a red T-shirt smarter, nicer and more fun than the children with a blue T-shirt. Their 'in group' was good, the other group was bad.

This is a very well-known social phenomenon which some sport clubs and student organizations make good use of. When a new class signs up, they put them in the same clothes and let them carry out some difficult tasks. Thereafter, everyone in the group

----

* An article by Nass, Steurer, Henriksen and Dryer describes that humans, when they evaluate machines, react in the same way as when they evaluate humans. They respond to the same social norms. See: Nass, Steuer, Henriksen & Dryer, 1994.

** This research is covered in great detail in Tajfel, 1982. But there are many more examples illustrating the same principle. See for example: Mackie, 1986; Myers & Lamm, 1976.

likes each other, and they have developed an aversion to people outside the group.

This 'group polarization' effect was also examined by Reeves and Nass. Of course that was quite difficult, because computers do not normally wear T-shirts. The researchers found the following solution: half the participants in their study received a red T-shirt and carried out a task with a computer with a red monitor. During the task, participants were told that they were the 'red team', together with their computer. The other half of the participants received a blue T-shirt, while the computer had a red monitor. They were not told that they were a team, but they had to carry out the same task.

After the task, participants were again asked to rate the computer – this time on a different computer, because the researchers knew that people would provide a fairer evaluation that way. As it turned out, the participants evaluated the performance of the computer with a monitor that shared the color of their own T-shirt higher than the participants who were not wearing a shirt the same color as the computer. They felt they were part of the same team. The feedback from the computer was more useful and the proposed information more correct if they were a team. At least, that's what the participants indicated: in reality the computer gave the exact same advice during the task.

The above studies show that people cannot shield themselves from their psychological reactions. The responses we have developed for human-to-human communication mostly have an evolutionary basis. Once, at a time when we were hunters and gatherers, it was a very good idea to trust the people in your group and distrust those outside. Since those ancient times we simply have not had enough time, on the evolutionary scale, to develop new reactions to computers and other interactive media.

Persuasive technology

If computers can use the same psychological persuasion principles as humans, then theoretically there is no good reason why the impact should decrease as the reach of our communication grows. Perhaps the decrease in impact is observed only because our cur-

rent computers – in the ways we have programmed them – are bad
influencers. Theoretically, we should be able to construct computers or other interactive media that are able to create a big impact.

Professor BJ Fogg, who worked with Reeves and Nass early
on, was one of the first to understand this. Based on his insights,
he wrote a book called *Persuasive Technologies: How Computers
Change What We Think and Do.** In his book Fogg describes three
ways in which computers and interactive media can direct our behavior. Firstly, computers can make things easier, so we do those
things more often. Since we no longer have go out into the rain
with the advent of online stores, we might be more inclined to visit
them.

Secondly, computers or interactive media can explain things
just like people. Through simulation, we can experience what it's
like to exhibit certain behaviors. We see in a video how easy it is
to make an online purchase and therefore we are likely to do it
ourselves.

Finally, BJ Fogg links back to the research of his previous men-
tors: computers and interactive media can, if they try to influence
people, use the same psychological and social processes as people.
Even interactive systems can therefore actively use persuasion to
influence human behavior.

Following the publication of BJ Fogg's book, several researchers
started to study and develop interactive media, and other interactive systems that had the intention of influence the behavior of their
users. Researchers now create websites that encourage people to stop
smoking and smart phone applications that measure how much a
user exercises, in order to coach them into a healthier lifestyle.

In his later work Fogg not only affirmed the idea that computers can influence people but added explicitly that they can actually

---

*   The book by BJ Fogg initiated a research field that now encompasses
hundreds of researchers. The book is an easy read and a great starting point
for this area. See: Fogg, 2002. Professor Fogg was, after the publication of
his book, one of the first to recognized the importance of mobile technology
for *persuasive technology*. See Fogg & Eckles, 2007. Right now professor
Fogg mainly focuses on the use of technology to create long-term behavioral
change (see for example Fogg, 2009).

have an even bigger impact than humans. This is contrary to our earlier conclusions – that computers inherently have less impact than people and that therefore the effect does not increase linearly with reach. In human-to-human communication, information storage and collection by the influencer is limited: a seller recognizes you only if you are a frequent customer, and often will not remember all the details of your previous purchases. Computers and smart phones however can do much more: they can measure everything, and they can store anything for indefinite periods of time. In addition, computers and smart phones can influence you at all times: they can interrupt you again and again, draw your attention to something, and potentially influence you. Whereas you can likely escape a salesperson, you are unlikely to turn off your phone.

Summarizing

Instead of using theories to explain why impact decreases as reach grows, we need to find out what we are doing wrong: why do we create bad influencers? And, more importantly, how can we increase impact while maintaining reach?

Increasing impact is an important goal of researchers engaged in the development of persuasion technologies. But marketers too are working hard to increase the impact of their online stores, while the reach remains the same. In recent years, impact has steadily increased, while reach has remained unchanged. In the rest of this book I will demonstrate how impact has recently increased, and how I believe we will increase it even more in the next decade.

In this chapter we talked about impact: the influence that people (or machines) have on the decision-making process of others. We also talked about reach: the number of people being 'addressed' by another person. Impact and reach together determine the effect of the influencer. I have explained that, although our reach has grown enormously because of mass media and the Internet, the impact has only decreased, and therefore, the effect has not been significant. So:

- In the past (and even now when speaking about human to human interaction) people had a great influence on each other. A salesperson could significantly influence the decision-making process of a buyer and a good debater could change the opinion of an opponent.
- After we started to comprehend impact, we got access to technology which increased our reach. With each novel communication technology, the number of people a single person could reach increased.
- Right now a single person can reach the entire world.
- In our enthusiasm about the increase in reach we forgot about impact. We were talking to millions of people, but nobody was listening.
- Communication researchers, marketers, and other scientists are starting to focus more on increasing impact.
- Because humans react the same way to computers as to other humans, computers could have the same impact as people had in the past.
- Theoretically, computers could even have a higher impact than humans: They can remember everything and are always 'on'.

3

FIRST YOU HAVE TO BE FOUND

Hawaii means beautiful weather so I also needed swimming trunks. It is however winter in the Netherlands (where I happen to live at this moment). I leave the bookstore and of course, it's raining. I fasten my coat, jump on my bike and continue to the nearest store that might still have swimming trunks available.

Totally drenched I enter the store. Cold and wet I look around and conclude that the range of swimming trunks in the average sporting goods store in the Netherlands in late December leaves much to be desired. It is however still raining outside so I'd rather not cycle to the next store.

I look at three pairs of swimming trunks but none of them are to my liking. One of the three is not extremely ugly – just moderately ugly. And it is also very attractively priced. And, since it's fairly ugly, it is likely to be a fairly rare item: I often like things that are scarce. I could of course go to another store… on the other side of town, but that would make me even wetter and colder than I already am. And I don't really rate the chance that they will have a more suitable collection as good.

A sales clerk approaches me: 'Remarkable item isn't it?' A somewhat sarcastic smile betrays that he shares my taste.

I decide to buy them anyway. I assume that I can still buy some in Hawaii but I don't want to risk missing the first surfing session the evening I arrive because I only have my underwear available.

On the way home I think about my pretty ridiculous purchase. How is it that I occasionally come home with very ugly stuff? On-line I probably would have been able to find something that fit my taste perfectly, and if the first online store did not have anything available then it would not have taken a lot of effort to go to the next store. Comfortably sitting on the couch, with some help from Google, I could have surfed comfortably from shop to shop, while outside it rained on.

One day before leaving for Hawaii, this wasn't a viable option for me, But it is a good example of the loss of impact while the reach is expanding. For each of the online stores that I would have visited from my comfortable position on the couch in my living room I would have been a potential customer. I would have count-ed towards their total reach despite the fact that I would never have bought something in every store. Since it is so easy to digi-tally 'walk' from shop to shop I probably would have contributed towards the total reach of ten or so shops. However, I would, at the most, have made a purchase which would count towards total effect from only one of them Compare this with the experience in the single offline store. Even with a hideous swimsuit and a sarcas-tic sales clerk, they had an impact, and therefore ultimately had effect. That shop successfully sold the swimming trunks.

Although this book focuses primarily on increasing impact by applying psychological sales principles, I first want to pay some at-tention to the growth of the reach of online media, and the differ-ences between online and offline visitors. Those differences partly explain the lack of impact (as we saw in the previous chapter) and are therefore important in our final analysis.

THE YELLOW PAGES

There were times – long gone – when, if we wanted to find a spe-cific store, we looked in a big book: The yellow pages. In this book, the various shops and businesses in our vicinity were neatly ar-ranged according to subject and city. If you wanted to find some swimming trunks and were not familiar with the city you were in, you just opened the book to the sports section and searched for the right address. Next you looked up the address on the map that was conveniently printed in the same book. Then, you set out by car or bike to find the store using your own perfect sense of direction.

Of course, there were also situations in which you already knew the name of the right shop or chain store to buy your swimming trunks from. If this was the case, then you could use an alphabetical index to find the address of your preferred store. This index was simply an ordered overview of all listed companies.

In the previous chapter, I explained how total reach expanded during the transition from human-to-human communication to communication through books and other media, and ultimately the Internet, I actually glossed over the way in which these books and web pages would find their way to you. Theoretically the reach was continuously growing. However, you needed to have access to the books or to the Internet before the theoretical reach became a reality.

The way in which the total reach increased has contributed to the decline in impact. For example, a greater reach by several service providers means that it has become easier for you as a consumer to switch providers. If I do not have to go out on my bike into the rain to find new swimming trunks, I will more easily switch to search for a suitable product in some other store. The easier it is to reach vendors, the smaller the impact per vendor will become. This relationship between reach and impact has also been studied scientifically: as early as 1991 Lynn pointed out that there is a relationship between the amount of effort people have to put into finding a product and their willingness to buy it. Products that are very easily available everywhere don't often turn out to be the products that everyone wants, or that people much appreciate. A little more effort often leads to increased intent to purchase, and ultimately to a greater willingness to pay.[*]

---

[*] A considerable body of scientific literature is available on the effects of scarcity, the amount of effort that consumers put into finding the right product, and the effects on purchase intention. Lyn presents an overview (particularly related to the effects of scarcity) in: Lyn, 1991.

YOUR UNIQUE NAME MAKES YOU STAND OUT

When the Internet was still in its infancy, the theoretical possibility of achieving growth in reach soon became clear. One could write something and the writing would instantly be visible to anyone with a dial-up connection. One could put something up for sale and anyone in the world could, in theory, buy it. But it was not quite as simple as that. It was not as if everyone read everything that was published on the Internet or bought everything that was offered for sale. First consumers had to find you.

Usually new technology imitates the old before it becomes clear what new possibilities and applications the new technology has to offer. Initially, if you wanted to read my publications or to buy something from me, you had to know the address of my online store. You typed the address directly into your browser to reach my store or my writings. At that moment the theoretical great reach of the new medium had not yet been achieved. In fact you first had to reach someone face-to-face to get the right address. This would soon change however.

TOP LISTS AND CATEGORIES

The real internet as we know it, with its fantastic reach but low impact, was introduced by Tim Berners Lee, and the real breakthrough consisted mainly of the idea of hyperlinks: a way to refer from one online page to the next. It was already possible to retrieve information from another computer by typing in an address on your own computer. Now it became possible to easily put multiple addresses together in one place and to direct people with hardly any effort from one place to the next.

It did not take long before the yellow pages started to be imitated on the Internet. In some places on the Internet, lists – or indexes – of all web pages started to appear. These lists were often arranged by topic and offered visitors the opportunity to find information quickly. It is precisely at this time that the reach of online pages started to grow. For instance, consumers could now find the information I had written easily, or even the online store I had set up. They could reach me without knowing the address and without leaving their comfortable chairs. The list replaced the need for an easy to remember address.

The indexes increased the reach considerably and were in fact the first real steps in the direction of achieving the theoretical reach. Several parties made indexes: some created by people and some computer generated. Computers actually searched the web, classified the webpages they encountered, and ordered them automatically into indexes. Some of the first companies that produced these indexes later became the most powerful Internet companies of our time: Yahoo! is an example of this.

With the emergence of indexes, it really became clear that total reach was growing indeed. Unfortunately, impact was in rapid decline at the same time. Pages were increasingly being visited, but they were not being read attentively. The first attempts at online sales had little success despite the considerable number of visitors. The ease of reach had in fact changed something: people who were reached never intended to buy. They were simply exploring the bright new wonders of the then new Internet.

The search engine: a list of lists

I just mentioned that indexes were made both by humans as well as, increasingly, by computers. This was done using robots: robots travelled along all Internet addresses,* collected information on the pages they found and subsequently put that information in the index. In this way indexes were not only made automatically, they were also continually growing. Yet, in many ways they were also getting worse at the same time: while more and more pages were added – everyone wanted to take advantage of the fantastic reach – it became ever more difficult to see the wood for the trees. Because of the slight chaos that started to arise the effect, through the combination of reach and impact, was not very large. There were just too many sites and there was too much pulp.

The indexes, and their clutter, gave rise to search engines as

---

* Most 'bots' travel the Internet by following all the links listed on webpages. Technically this is very easy to accomplish. It is however not the case that you can only be found based on the links to your website. Most indexes and search engines nowadays offer the opportunity to list your own webpages directly.

we use them today. The first search engines were actually nothing more than a quick way to navigate through the existing index, but they were quickly becoming ever more sophisticated. The goal increasingly became to ensure that a potential visitor to a web page indeed landed where he or she wanted to arrive. By ensuring a good fit of the visitor to the page, it would not only have a greater reach, but perhaps also have real impact. This would generate at least some effect if people were looking for your product.

A variety of ways were developed in order to channel the reach. Yahoo!, one of the first indexes, for example, has experimented for some time with the determination of the rank; the position of a page in the list of results which is generated after a search, This sometimes on the basis of how deep the pockets of the webpage owner were. If you paid more, you scored higher and your name appeared higher on the list.

Soon the competition started (e.g. Google) and they used other ways to rank pages in an index. Eventually, of course, the goal was to recommend a page that matched what the visitor was looking for. In this way the page would not only enjoy a wide reach but also a large impact. So those who made indexes tried to determine the importance of the page in relation to the search query. In the beginning it was simple: if a search term appeared on the page then it came at the top of the search results. Soon this was true however for hundreds of pages, and another way had to be found to rank the pages. Additionally, more and more website builders -- all in search of reach – started to add all possible words to their pages in order to be found – even though the page was unrelated to the subject of the search. These website builders assumed that a gigantic reach, regardless of impact, would always produce some effect.

ATTRACTING THE RIGHT PEOPLE

The biggest breakthrough in finding the right page for the visitor was Pagerank.* This algorithm was developed by Larry Page and Sergey Brin and is based on the following simple but ingenious

---

* The very first version of the Pagerank algorithm is described in Page, Brin, Rajeev, & Winograd, 1999.

idea: if someone surfs the web at random and clicks on a link he encounters, how great would the chance of him landing on any given page be? As more pages are linked to a particular page, the chances of randomly landing on that specific page become larger, and therefore it should have a higher ranking in the list. The more important the website is on the web – measured by the number of links to that page from other pages – the higher up the page should be in the search results.

Nowadays almost every search engine uses this idea, and the order of many search results is therefore largely determined by the number of other pages that link to a page. These links to a page are called 'backlinks'. * Current search engines however use many more variables: the text on the website and the number of back-links are no longer the only criteria to score high – although they are still among the most important. Google claims currently to use more than 200 features (criteria) to determine whether a site should rank high or low in the search results, and other search algorithms claim to use at least as many. This makes it increas-ingly difficult for website builders to 'cheat' the search results by changing their content, text, or backlinks. The opportunities to artificially boost reach by fooling the search engines have lately decreased, and in turn this has increased the impact of the pages that have a really good score.

Ranking high in search engines and indexes is an art in itself and it is worthwhile: guiding the right visitors to your page will lead to both reach and impact. Attracting the right visitor is of great im-portance to realizing online effect. This has led to the rise of many companies that are specialized in so-called search engine optimi-zation (SEO). They assist companies in designing their websites in such a way that they maximize the scoring possibilities on all of the two hundred criteria. Not only to obtain a high index score, but specifically to attract the right people: people who are willing to take action, by which both impact and reach are guaranteed.

---

* *Backlink* is not the only term used. Other terms for the same pur-pose, such as *inbound link*, *inlink* and *incoming link,* are also used by marketers.

Within the current infrastructure, I think the theoretical reach of online media has almost been achieved. It is indeed possible to reach the world on your own! You will have to compete with all the others who are trying to do this, but even face-to-face your ideas and ultimate impact will also depend on the behavior of other influencers. My only fear is that – despite the efforts of the Googles and Yahoo!s of this world to attract the right visitors – the enlarged reach is still only reaching people with whom the impact is inherently lower. That by itself is the prime reason that the ultimate impact of online marketing is still disappointing based on reach alone.

Advertise and pay in order to be found

In addition to search engine optimization – SEO – there is also a lot of attention on SEA: search engine advertising. This actually links back to the old idea of Yahoo!: let people pay for their place in the final index. Today, however, most search engines do not offer the opportunity to appear in the actual search results but right next to or above them. Again, the priority is to increase the reach – if you have paid to be on the front page, next to the 'real' search results, then the reach will indeed be large. But the impact is of course also important: you should ensure that your advertisement – because that is what it is in the end – is shown to the right people: people who are actually looking for your service or product. To achieve all this, it is currently possible to bid on certain keywords: if someone is searching for 'insurance', then you can pay to appear on the first results page, thus ensuring you reach people with whom you hope to finally achieve an impact. That is, if you sell insurance. The challenge will mainly be to select the right message – the right end goal – to achieve impact.

Most search engines use a kind of auction to allow one to advertise in combination with a particular search term. In its simplest form you as an insurance provider can announce that you are interested in advertising on the front page of the search results for the term insurance, and you can specify how much money you have available for a click on your advertisement. Other insurance providers can do the same, and the search engine will ensure that it will show the ad belonging to the highest bidder at all times in order to maximize their own profit.

Because of this bidding system it has become an art to optimize the effect of the SEA for a small amount of money. The service or product provider will search for the right terms which they know potential customers tend to use before buying the product. But it must also be a search term that is preferably not used by competitors. If there is no competition then the bids will be low and one can obtain a wide reach for the smallest amount of money. On the other hand, it still has to be a term which occurs often enough to ensure sufficient reach. Balancing all these variables is a skill that some SEA companies do indeed possess. Increasingly companies are trying to reach those people who will ultimately be willing to make a purchase: the limited value of blind reach is becoming obvious.

A similar system of bidding is not only used to advertise on search results pages, but is also used for banner advertisements. Many websites – or rather their owners – make a living from the fact that they show ads alongside the (useful) content of their websites. These ads are often traded in the same way as the positions next to the search results: you, the advertiser, can bid for an exposure to a visitor on a given site on a particular topic. Here too it is an art to ensure that the advertisement is displayed on a website where the impact is as high as possible, for as little money as possible.

A final development, which aims to reduce blind reach and increase impact by ensuring that the right customer finds the right product, is 'behavioral targeting'. Although quite complicated versions of behavioral targeting exist, the basic idea is very simple. Suppose you are looking for information about cycling using a search engine. This search term is remembered. If afterwards you visit the website of your favorite bookstore, it will show you books about cycling on its home page. The ultimate goal of this attempt to influence you is to adapt the content of the communication based on your previous behavior. Behavioral targeting is an important recent step in selecting the right product for the right customer. But even with behavioral targeting, the effect is often still limited.

EMAIL & SPAM

So far, I have focused on the growth of reach due to the rise of the Internet, and the subsequent decline of impact that this led to. Then I explained how SEO and SEA influencers are currently trying to 'steer' reach in such a way that impact can still be achieved. When you attract the right audience, you are more likely to convince people more effectively thus leading to a greater effect.

But there is more to the web than web pages. Other forms of digital communication have gone through similar evolutions; email, for example. The theoretical reach of email was immediately clear and attractive to influencers. It took only a few moments before virtually everyone had an email address.

Once this was a reality, the reach seemed fantastic. It was possible for influencers to buy lists with email addresses so they could approach millions of people at the same time.* But here, too, the impact declined in spectacular fashion as soon as the reach increased. The more emails that were sent to influence readers the less they were read and the more often they were considered as spam: messages people were not waiting for. Meanwhile spam – basically unwanted attempts to influence – is largely automatically intercepted. By this I don't just mean the ones that are in your own spam box, but the ones you don't even get to see. These comprise over 80% of all incoming emails.

Recently the impact of email has been on the rise again. To paint you a picture of what is currently possible in this area, let me share my experiences of the Design for Conversion conference a couple of years ago in Ghent, Belgium. This is only one example. In the next chapter we will go into more depth on the current possibilities for increasing online impact, but also the mistakes that are still regularly made. We make mistakes because we still find it

---

* To the best of my knowledge this is still possible. It is a somewhat questionable way to earn money, but apparently it is difficult to stop due to inadequate regulation. The impact is often very small, but due to the extremely high reach there still is a small effect. Achieving such small effects, whilst irritating countless other people who don't require Viagra or penis enlargements, seems to be of little consequence to their providers.

hard to really understand how to influence impact.

If you are not into email marketing or do not know the technical details of an email marketing action, this might be some new information for you. When a company sends an email to its customers, it is technically possible to change the content after it has been sent. Some parts of the actual content of the email are in fact only retrieved at the moment the recipient opens the email.

Imagine that I open my email before you open the same email. The company that sent it to me can track how I respond to the email (do I order the product?) and can decide to change the content of the email sent to you on that basis; from the very moment I open it. This technology allows for the possibility of creating and using three (or more) versions of an email. The company that sends the emails can then keep track of which version results in the highest sales, the highest number of clicks or whatever else it wants. The company can then decide to show the version of the email that worked best for all early openers to those that open their mail at a later time. Overall the reach remains the same in this case – the mail is still sent to millions of potential customers – but the version of the email with the highest impact can be determined automatically.*

One of the speakers at the Design for Conversion conference was the founder of the company that made the ability described above technically possible. His presentation made it clear to me that increasing impact online is still in its infancy. He talked about the fantastic technical possibilities of customizing the email while responses were arriving. And of course he also described some of the success stories: situations where this technology had led to surprising results. He described how they had organized a major email marketing program for a big telecom provider. This company was offering a new type of subscription. The marketers had

---

* This is known as a type of A-B testing (more about this in the next chapter). There are a few problems (mainly statistical and methodological) with this kind of testing. Its fundamentals are sound however. The marketer probably doesn't really know in advance which version will work best and therefore it is good idea to determine this empirically.

decided to offer a gift to their prospective customers to entice them
to sign up. They were not sure however which of those gifts, a new
smartphone or an in-home draught beer system, would be more
effective. So they decided to test these two versions of the email:
one containing the smartphone as a gift and the other containing
the draught beer system. But before the speaker revealed the results to us he asked the audience which gift they thought would be
more successful. The response was almost unanimous: the smartphone. This was a fairly logical choice, since the smartphone was
about twice as expensive as the draught beer system and potential
customers, if clever, could have chosen to take the smartphone,
sell it and then buy two draught systems for the money they had
received.

And then came the surprise. Of the first 10,000 people who
had opened the mail 5,000 were presented with the draught beer
system and the other 5,000 with the smartphone. The result? The
email with the draught beer system was almost twice as effective as
the email with the smartphone! The email was therefore adapted
and – automatically – the rest of the recipients got the offer for the
draught beer system.

This was indeed a surprising example of the possibilities of increasing online impact. But of all the examples that the speaker
could have chosen this was the worst one in my eyes. The method
of testing emails as described above happens to have one big weak-
ness: it implicitly assumes that the first 10,000 people who open
the email react the same as the 990,000 people that follow. Now
I do believe that this will often be the case, and that the method
is useful. However, this is absolutely not the case in his example. Quite simply, the first 10,000 people who opened the mail
were probably able to do that because they had direct access to
their emails. Logically these recipients already had a smartphone!
Therefore, it was logical that a majority of these early openers
would choose the draught beer system. However, this might not
be the case for the subsequent 990,000 email readers who did not
own a smartphone.

NETWORK EFFECTS

So marketers have found ways to attract more visitors, ensure that these are the right visitors and present them with the right results. This still leaves open the case of the so-called social networks. Those are pretty hip right now, and as I will not go into these in great detail in the rest of my book it might be a good idea to briefly address them at this point.

A few years ago many consumers joined a social network (this used to be Hyves in the Netherlands, but is now just Facebook like everywhere else). The reach – and the potential impact – of these social networks is huge. The lack of psychological influencing being used on these networks is, in my opinion, an important reason for the lack of effect they have at this time. There are, however, two phenomena that I explicitly want to introduce. These are important for understanding the potential effects that persuasion can have in digital environments.

The first phenomenon is 'contagion': the contagion of ideas in social networks. The idea is pretty simple: you have a number of friends on Facebook or another social network. Suppose someone from outside has influenced your opinion on some subject. You in turn are now likely to influence the people around you, which in turn will affect others. Thus, the influence exerted on you becomes contagious. Eventually your opinion might infect the whole social network.* It goes 'viral'!

However, many concepts eventually do not go viral; they do not seem so contagious at all. Behavioral scientists are trying to understand why some ideas are contagious and others are not. The first scientific models for understanding the effects of a virus came from biology. The spread of an idea through a social network has many things in common with the way a virus spreads

---

* From 'contagion' comes the idea of a *viral*, a word that is often used for videos (not exclusively) that go 'viral' and spread themselves like a virus. An example of this is the Ice Bucket challenge which went viral around the World quite recently. The different methods of making ads go viral are now also the subject of scientific studies. See for instance Golan & Zaidner, 2008.

amongst a group of people. Because of the emergence of social media, researcher into the contagious effects of communication has become very popular. Studies have been conducted into how different types of ideas spread, but also into the influence of the structure of the network and how this structure affects contagion.

Some of the best research in this field comes from Sinan Aral, Lev Muchnik and Arun Sundararajan. These three researchers specifically studied impact in social networks and showed how ideas spread through a network. They tested the old marketing idea that there are certain people who have more influence, so they are more infectious than others. In their simulation study, the researchers showed that these influential people could indeed exist and could provide the first infections of a network with an idea: they could create impact. But they also showed the following: if you as an influencer could influence a coherent group in a network – say, you and all your friends – then the chance of contamination of the whole network was often much greater than when you focused on the influential only. Aral, Muchnik and Sundararajan thus showed that changing the opinion of a 'cluster' -- a group with many connections – in a network is more effective than 'influentials' in the network. This is a surprising conclusion, because it is contrary to marketing ideas that have prevailed for years. But in my view the study does show that we are only at the beginning in the field of online impact, including impact in social networks. We still have to greatly expand our knowledge about the real causes of impact.*

The same researchers discovered another striking finding. In 2009, they focused on the question of whether contagion in a social network is caused by the effect of one person on another -- so-called peer influence effects -- or rather by the underlying fact that people who are friends probably have similar interests and therefore do the same things. In this case it might appear as if someone's

---

* The source of this idea is in the fantastic work on the adoption of innovations by Rogers (1995). His book wasn't a marketing book at all but his ideas were so powerful that they still influence marketers today.

behavior leads a friend to do the same, but the friend wouldn't the friend have done it anyway?*

Until this study many scientists assumed that the effect of peer influence – I see my friend do something so I do it too – was very great. There were already studies available on social networks that showed that as the number of your friends who shared a link or 'liked' a page increased, your tendency to share that link also increased. Nobody doubted the strength of peer influence. However, the researchers did something very clever to nuance this truth. They hid the fact from some of the people in their study that their friends were actually sharing a link or liking a page. Therefore there was no peer influence – the researcher turned it off. But this could happen under normal circumstances.

The results were amazing: even if you do not see that your friend like a page, you are still inclined to do the same. It is not peer influence that is taking place – after all you cannot even see what your peers are doing. What is really happening is a phenomenon called 'homophily': you do the same as your friends because you have a similar background. Almost half of the effect of peer influence could in fact be explained by homophily!

Social networks, which are emerging fast, offer some of the best ways to achieve a very high reach. Yet on these networks, the theoretical effect are far from being realized. I hope the above two examples (on contagion and homophily) illustrate that we still have a poor understanding of impact within social networks. Our current marketing knowledge on the distribution of products and ideas in networks is likely insufficient. However, is the good news is that it's getting better. Social networks provide scientists, such as Aral, Muchnik and Sundararajan, with an opportunity to undertake studies that can help us better to understand how we create impact.

----

* This concerns a simulation study but it shows convincingly that network effects can be more important than the effect of a specific type of individual. See Aral, Muchnik & Sundararajan, 2009.

WHERE ARE WE?

Search engines have helped us to reach the right people and consequently have partially increased the impact that was lost when the number of websites and amount of information exploded. This puts us in a situation where – for the first time – it has become possible to have a huge effect. However, this effect doesn't happen very often. We reach the right people, and we understand somewhat how messages spread through networks, but we are still far away from the good sales clerk in terms of actual impact. As described in the case of e-mail, the possibilities for testing the potential impact of different content is the next step. But current studies do not deal with issues that are psychologically of great interest. The fact that the in-home draught beer system may then on average have more effect than the smartphone, doesn't actually provides us with information about consumers that we can reuse in the future. This type of testing does not often tell us why something has an impact or not.

This chapter has highlighted the efforts – often valuable – that have been made to fully utilize the potential reach of the Internet. The effects however are still very disappointing. In the next chapter I will try to describe how researchers and marketers have tried, in recent years, to increase the effect of the Internet.

SUMMARIZING

In this chapter I have tried to outline the ways in which we have managed to increase the reach of online media. But I have also demonstrated how this, at the same time, has led to lower impact. We reach a lot of people, but these people are less likely to be affected. Search engines have partly resolved this problem by ensuring that the right providers reach the right people. This has also been happening in email marketing. I have also presented an example of contemporary testing methods to increase the impact throughout the media channels. Finally, I have shown how impact is achieved in social networks, which will eventually have a reach and impact that may be even greater than those of the traditional media. A short summary:

- Despite the wide reach of digital communication, the effect is often limited.
- Initially, the effect was limited because there was too much content, so the messages did not reach the right people.
- Search engines have resolved this problem to some extent, so it is now possible to have a wide reach among consumers and a large impact as well.
- SEAs and SEOs are currently the main instruments for attracting the right people.
- In addition to SEOs and SEAs testing increasingly takes place to see the effect of different messages, so they can be optimized.
- When a website was found using the right search terms, online marketers further concentrated on improving impact by selecting the right products and the right way of offering them.

4

RECOMMENDER SYSTEMS: THE FIRST ATTEMPT AT ONLINE PERSUASION

Daniel Dennett, a philosopher who has authored many influential books on evolution, once wrote about the largest library in the world. Dennet envisioned a library that would contain all the books we could ever think of. It would not just contain all existing books to date; no, it would contain all possible books: past and future.

If you picked the first book from the shelves of this library, it would begin with only the letter A. No words, no story, just the letter A repeated for pages on end. The second book is almost identical to the first, but it contains, somewhere within, a different letter. Somewhere in the second book there is a B.

If you walk through the library, you will find that it is gigantic. It contains books with only As and 2 Bs, 3 Bs, 4 Bs, a C, etc. And with one letter being changed at a time, and this process being continued book after book, the library thus contains all possible books that can ever be written. Dennet's library contains the book that you are reading right now and it was there even before I wrote it.

In practice, of course, libraries are not filled this way since a) the library would become unimaginably large, and b) because of the large number of books it would be impossible to find a book that was actually worthwhile reading. However, it's an intriguing idea.

Dennett's library immediately came to mind when I first used Amazon.com a number of years ago. The stock of this online store is so vast that it is difficult to find the products you might want to purchase and this nowadays seems to be true for many other online stores. Many people believe that a large stock makes it easier to find things, but Den-

nett's library shows that this is not always the case. * *Using the language
we developed in the previous chapters, we could safely conclude that
Dennett's library would have little impact. If you could never find a
book you liked, you would probably never borrow a book defeating the
purpose of libraries. The effect of the gigantic library would be minimal indeed..*

The previous chapter described how the reach of online communication has increased over the last few years while the impact
seemed to have faded at the same time. This would imply that
the total effect of our online communication seems rather limited.
This might in some part be due to the fact that many of the people
that are reached are just not willing to be influenced. However,
it seems that even when we reach the right people, the impact remains rather low.

Accordingly, the next step towards increasing the effect of online
communication is to increase the impact of each attempt. Once
'hungry' customers have found your online store, how do you make
sure that they actually purchase your products? Before we discuss
psychological means to improve impact (chapter 5) let's first discuss
the attempts of marketers and engineers to overcome the problem
of Dennett's Library: how do we make sure that hungry customers find the products that appeal to them? This chapter discusses
recommender systems and several other attempts to improve the
impact of online selling through personalization and testing.

FINDING THIS BOOK IN DENNETT'S LIBRARY

Once you have entered an online store – which means that you
have just been reached – the question that arises is how do we sellers generate impact? How do we influence you to make an actual
purchase?

As we discussed before, these attempts often fail. In part this
is because the online store is decorated differently than the offline

---

* As I stated before, there is a great deal of research that shows that extra
choice does not necessarily make things easier for people. See for example:
White & Hoffrage, 2009.

store, so the ultimate impact is necessarily different. Initially, however, marketers believed that by offering a huge range of products, online stores would quickly outperform offline ones. Although a large stock provides the buyer with many options, online stores with huge stocks initially seemed to inhibit rather than improve sales. Apparently many customers could not find the product they were looking for despite the online store carrying their preferred products,. The earliest attempts to increase impact in online selling ended up focusing on exactly this problem: How do we allow customers to navigate our online store and find the products that they are looking for? This challenge was largely different from offline equivalents: some online stores carry over 1,000,000 products which is unheard of in offline stores. Being able to navigate and easily find the desired products becomes of huge importance in increasing the impact of online selling.

The first and simplest solution to browsing a large number of products was to arrange the products in distinct product categories: We sell CDs, books, and DVDs. And on the first page one you have to choose which one you prefer. After choosing the CDs, for example, you can choose different musical genres, and then subgenres. As your choices get more and more detailed, you will eventually end up exactly at the product you require.

The category system, while sensible, has numerous problems. Take a band like Coldplay, are they pop? Rock? Britpop? And even if you as a seller can answer the question, then you are missing the point: each and every customer needs to answer these questions in the exact same way to make sure they all eventually arrive at the music album they are looking for. If your categories do not match those of a potential buyer, the category system is bound to lessen your impact.

When the categories are unclear, they can make life really difficult. And there are additional problems to the category structure: If you have millions of products, then the branches* of the catego-

---

* By 'branches of the tree' I am referring to the end point of a tree structure in which hierarchically ordered content can be placed. This is called a tree diagram.

ry tree are bound to get very thick: Even within CDs => pop => Britpop there might be thousands of albums. Categorization, our first attempt at solving the problem of too large an assortment, is thus hard to implement effectively in practice: it is hard to find a structure which matches the mental model of your customers.*

After trying out classification trees and other category structures, many online sellers switched to adding search functionality to their website. Searches allowed the customer looking for a Coldplay album to directly type 'Coldplay' into a little text field at the top of the online store and find all the products related to Coldplay. If done well, searches can make it possible to find almost any product one wants directly. Search functionality subsequently increased the impact of many online stores: adding a search field increased their conversion rates. However, the increase was limited to a distinct group of customers: those who know in advance exactly what they are looking for. Search completely eliminated the opportunity to stumble upon new product suggestions.** Where a tree structure might not lead a customer to finding Coldplay, at least they would find other pop or Britpop albums – whichever branch of the category tree they ended up traversing. Not so with simple search: only those products matching 'Coldplay' exactly would be displayed. This decreases the chance of impulse buying of other products that belong to a similar category.

PERSONALIZATION
Paralleling the rise of searches, personalization of webpages appeared: the technical ability to show you a different page from your neighbor when visiting the same site. Even for the exact same search terms, you and your neighbor could be confronted with different pages. While the goal of personalization attempts was often to sell more by letting you find your potential products more easily, not all attempts focused on selling directly: some websites

---

*   The mental model of the customer can heavily affect the subsequent interaction. For a discussion on this see: Allen, 1997.
**   Many designers of interactive products believe that the ability to stumble upon new ideas and products is extremely important to retain in digital environments. See Danzico, 2010, for further discussion.

would welcome me by saying 'Hello Maurits': a very personal and touching experience.

Personalization of online communication, and its effects, began to make its mark in around 2000. People started becoming aware of the fact that the ads they were seeing were adapted to their previous behavior: You searched for high-heeled shoes; you would get ads featuring high-heeled shoes.

Initially however the personalization was not always done well: it is technically not an easy task. In 2002, Jeffrey Zaslow wrote a great article in the Wall Street Journal about TiVo entitled 'My TiVo Thinks I Am Gay'.* TiVo was a popular set-top box, which allowed consumers to watch television and movies on demand. TiVo made it possible to watch television shows when it suited you, the user, instead of at times that suited advertisers and broadcasters. The extremely large variety of programs and films available through TiVo changed the experience of watching television.

TiVo personalized the movie selection page of its users, and it was one of the first to do so. Each user was presented with a set of potentially interesting films. These interesting films were selected for each individual viewer, and TiVo decided whatever was interesting. TiVo analyzed your previous viewing habits and behavior and would then recommend new movies. This, of course, is great! You get to discover new movies that you like. However, what happens when TiVo is wrong?

What do you do if TiVo mistakenly thinks you are gay? And continuously recommends films with homosexual elements? This exactly happened to Basil Iwanyk who was interviewed by Jeffrey in the 2002 article. In TiVo's mind, after a few days of interacting with Basil, Basil was gay. And thus, all the recommended movies would have a link to this topic.

TiVo was persistent. It took Basil many days of watching war movies and westerns, which he deemed non-gay, before TiVo changed its mind. However, the sudden burst of violent war movies put TiVo on the wrong foot again: Basil would then only be recommended movies about the Third Reich, Himmler, or other

---

* See http://online.wsj.com/article_email/SB1038261936872356908.html.

matters that Basil really did not want to be associated with. In Ti-Vo's mind Basil changed from friendly gay to a weird and aggressive war movie fanatic. To Basil, none of these typologies applied, making this one of the first clear failures of personalization.

OTHERS CUSTOMERS WHO BOUGHT THIS PRODUCT ALSO BOUGHT...

Although the article by Zaslow shows that personalization can often go wrong, it is still a step in the direction of higher impact. Personalization, both in ads as well as in product recommendations, has often been shown to increase the impact. The simplest form of personalization, one that is used by many online stores, is paradoxically not really based on you, but it is based on others like you. This method of personalization was pioneered by Amazon.com.

Amazon was looking for ways to recommend their products to clients: they were faced with the Dennett Library problem. For a new customer, Amazon would have no information available about preference, so it would be difficult to personalize your first experience. It would only be sensible to show new visitors a list of popular or best-selling products: these have a high chance of being liked by many. Many companies follow this strategy for new customers, but some opt for presenting the product they would like to see as bestselling as opposed to those that actually are bestsellers.

Now once you start browsing categories or searching the website your preferences become clearer. The online store can start compiling a profile of your preferences.

In practice however, this is not often not what is done. Personalization is not based on an elaborate profile of you, but rather on a very simple deduction: If you are viewing book A, and those who came before you and viewed book A ended up buying book B, then you will be recommended book B. The website does not even have to know what is in these books or to which category they belong: the behavior of earlier customers ultimately determines your 'personal' recommendations.

This simple way to recommend books (or other products) has been very successful for many online stores. It is also very easy for a computer to learn. Of course, it will not always be accurate. Occasionally you will be absolutely amazed by the ridiculous books that are recommended to you. But, in general, this simple idea works pretty well and often allows you to make great new discoveries. Thus, this method of personalization in part has solved the problems introduced by the search: The others who bought 'also-bought' recommendations made sure that the narrow search results were extended to include options for discovery and impulse buying.

The actual algorithm in use by Amazon and other successful e-commerce platforms will be a lot less simple than the one described above. It is likely to take more account of your previous behavior, and it will likely match you up with customers similar to you. And the algorithm will probably respect the vendor's business goals: If two products are available for recommendation, and one has a larger margin, then it makes business sense to recommend the product with the higher margin.

The first company to make personalization a hot topic of public debate was not Amazon: we seemed to like its recommendations and did not worry too much about them. In 2004, however, Gmail became available for the first time by invitation only and quickly became a very popular email provider. But Gmail was created by Google and it seemed to use whatever you wrote in your emails – or whatever you were sent – to personalize the ads that were in your next emails. It even seemed like the ads on Google's own search pages were informed by the things you had been discussing in emails. Had you received emails about cars, then you would find more cars everywhere. If you received an unwanted email about baby products or children's toys, then you were faced for days with endless toy commercials.

The link between the emails you had been reading and the ads you were seeing was glaring: and this was the first time the general public became aware of personalization. Initially, there was a lot of resistance: Google should not be allowed to 'read' the emails of its users. In reality, there was nobody reading the email: a machine read the emails, not a Google employee.

Public opinion about personalized advertisements changed

drastically after 2004. While Gmail's first attempts led to public uproar, nowadays companies like Facebook and Yahoo!, who both personalize their ads, get hardly any complaints about the fact that they apply personalization. Rather, they get complaints about the quality of their personalization: 'Would you please stop displaying ads for diapers? I am not yet ready to have babies...' Personalization itself seems to be fine, as long as it's done well.*

In recent years, the level of personalization of course has further increased. Your Facebook home page does not even resemble those of your friends: it is fully tailored to you. Actually, I believe many users of online stores still barely understand the extent to which web pages are personalized. While the personalization done by Gmail was relatively clear, the processes are now much more refined. You get products recommended because one of your friends 'liked' the product or solely because a mutual friend read a blog-post about the product. These types of personalization are a lot less evident than the direct link between your email content and the little ad next to it.

Algorithms and recommender systems

A lot of personalization is done using mathematical algorithms and models. These algorithms use different features, such as your click and search behavior or the behavior of others, to generate recommendations. The algorithms that are used to derive product recommendations are called recommender systems. The system that Amazon uses is an example.

A number of different types of personalization algorithms can be distinguished. First, there are algorithms that are based only on the relationships between products that have been observed by looking at previous visitors. Amazon's algorithm – or at least the first and most famous version – 'knew' nothing about a product itself: it relied only on the behavior of previous customers. Each

---

* This is not just a complaint I made up: a number of employees of both Facebook and Yahoo! that I spoke to remarked that the most often heard complaint about personalization concerned erroneous personalization, not the act of personalization itself.

product in the algorithm would just be a unique number, without any reference to the product's properties. If the same numbers were purchased together by many people then new visitors looking at one of these simple numbers would get the other one recommended. This means the algorithm had no theoretical understanding of why certain products were purchased together.* In these kinds of 'black–box' algorithms, the relationship between products is completely unknown to both computer and man. The disadvantage of this is that they cannot really deal with new products: if no previous purchase information is available, then the algorithm would never know when to recommend a new product. Since no one has ever bought the product in conjunction with another product, it will never be recommended.

On the other hand, an algorithm could be also based entirely on presupposed theoretical knowledge about people or products. For example, an algorithm could always recommend products that come from the same category: if you are interested in products from that category, other products belonging to the same category might also be of interest. The 'theory' regarding which products fall into which category is explicitly defined by humans. And, if this is known, then it is actually no longer necessary to collect data from consumers: the recommendation can be done purely

These theory-based recommendations sometimes go much further: there are companies that decide what type of customer you are based just on your first four clicks and the speed at which you move your mouse. And from then on you only see the information and products that the marketer considers relevant for you or, rather, your customer type. This is regardless of whether the strategy is actually effective and regardless of your further interactions with the website. So the algorithm makes an instantaneous choice about your customer type as specified by the marketer. There is no learning, nor a need to collect any additional data. What you get to see is dependent on no more data than

---

* The word 'theory' here might sound a bit bloated. However, I am referring not to scientific theories, but rather to a priori assumptions about human behavior.

your first four clicks and the theory of a marketer. This is very distinct from the black-box type algorithms which are fully data driven.

In addition to the distinction between data-driven and theory-driven personalization algorithms, there are other fundamental distinctions between algorithms: there are some that rely on the behavior of others and some that focus on your own behavior. In the past it was often only possible to generate recommendations based on the behavior of others who were more or less similar to you. Nowadays, as more people surf the Internet and all of their behavior is measured all the time, the personalization can be done directly based on your own past behavior.

It is quite obvious that a combination of approaches will ultimately be most effective: if you have no prior data about a product, you need to rely on theory to add it to recommendations. And, if you see a customer for the first time, it is fairly effective to rely on the observations obtained from other customers. Too often, however, people assume that what other similar people buy also applies to this particular individual – a mantra on which social psychology is almost entirety based. However, resistance to this view is increasing in the social sciences, and in practice it is increasingly clear that algorithms that include individual level behavior often generate better recommendations. *

Another meaningful distinction in personalization algorithms is between so-called dynamic and static systems. Static systems often divide visitors into distinct categories at some specific point in time. From that point onwards recommendations are based on the assigned category, and the category memberships remain the same for infinity. Dynamic systems, however, never make a final choice, and they change their 'opinion' with each response from a user. Every click you make and every product you buy will change the future recommendations. In theory, dynamic systems are more effective. However, they are not always practical to imple-

---

* In the last decade the idea that conclusions which hold on aggregate (over a group of people), will also hold for each individual has been disputed. See for example: Hutchinson, Kamakura & Lynch, 2001.

ment: dynamic systems often require more computer power and more maintenance. This is why truly dynamic algorithms are still hard to find in many organizations.

THE IMPORTANCE OF PERSONALIZATION

The importance of a good algorithm to generate recommendations was underlined in 2006 by Netflix, a company that provides access to digital films, series and television on demand. That year, Netflix announced the 'Netflix Challenge'.

The Netflix Challenge is aimed at improving their recommendation algorithm. Netflix customers are asked to give all the movies they watch a score of between 1 (total crap) and 5 (excellent). For those movies that a customer has not yet watched Netflix tries to predict their future scores so they can – potentially – recommend films that they feel are excellent. The algorithm is primarily based on the valuations of other customers for similar films. Since the actual business success of Netflix depends heavily on recommending films that you will indeed like, the estimates derived from the algorithm are of the utmost importance.

In 2006 Netflix published the evaluations of more than 400,000 customers for almost 18,000 movies. Besides these actual ratings, Netflix also published more than two million data points – which are movie-customer combinations – without any rating. Although the ratings for these additional 2 million data points were known to Netflix, they were just left out when they published the data. The challenge was simple: those who could write an algorithm which properly predicted the omitted ratings in the data set would receive a million dollars. There was one catch: the winning algorithm had to outperform Netflix's own algorithm.*

Netflix received hundreds of attempts for several years, and over the years the predictions got better. In the meantime, Netflix had ironically been awarded a prize for the worst algorithm.

---

* The prize was awarded based on a 10 percent improvement of the RMSE (Root Means Square Error (RMSE) as compared to Netflix's own algorithm. The RMSE is a measure for the deviance of the predicated score and the true score.

But by using smarter and smarter algorithms, the predictions improved. In 2009 Netflix awarded the million-dollar prize to a team of seven researchers who jointly submitted the best algorithm. The team had incorporated more than 500 variables in its final model, and used both a mix of the evaluations by others as well as lots of criteria obtained from the web. This final algorithm indeed beat Netflix's own recommendations.

Of course, almost all good recommender systems contain a combination of the factors I have described above. Most rely largely on data, but some theoretical understanding of the problem domain is necessary to specify the mathematical models. Good recommender systems use both individual data as well as the data from other customers. And almost all recommender systems in use by large companies who are specialists in the Internet domain are more or less dynamic nowadays.

Nevertheless, there is still a lot to do in the area of recommender systems. And some of the future developments are described in this book. We can, for instance, also distinguish recommender systems that focus on the end goal – the movie or other product that is recommended – from those that focus on the means by which that goal is attained. All of the examples discussed above have focused on selecting the right product and the right service, and thus on the end goal. But remember, the examples given in the previous chapters about offline selling should highlight that the way in which the end goal is pitched to customers can make a big difference. This is the future challenge for recommender systems. Adding the means to the end goal will increase the impact of online communication.

EASE OF USE

Recommendation systems that ensure that you find the products you might want have increased the impact of online communication. Once customers do find the product they are looking for, there are still a few more steps to take for a successful attempt to influence. While customers might like the product, and plan to buy it, all too often the deal is not closed online. You would for example think that placing a product in a shopping cart is a reasonable indicator of a customer's intention to buy. However, in 2011, 72 percent of the products placed in virtual shopping carts were not actually purchased.*

In order to solve this problem, online sellers have tried to generate impact not only by selecting the right products, but also by making the final check-out process easier. Many software professionals are concerned with making this, and other online processes, as easy as possible. They focus on what is called the 'usability' of interactive technologies. The logic behind this quest is trivial: if an online store is easy to use, it will be more likely to achieve a large net effect.

Usability, according to the theoretical accounts, is composed of a combination of effectiveness, efficiency, and satisfaction.** Effectiveness here refers to whether or not it is actually possible to carry out specific tasks. So, if you want to purchase a book at Amazon.com, this has to be possible without help. It should be intuitive to add the book to your shopping cart, fill out your credit card and address details, and order the product. Designers of e-commerce platforms use what they call usability testing to improve the overall usability of their websites. The test for effectiveness is quite simple: you put a customer in front of a website and ask them where they would click if they intended to buy a product. Often designers use the think-aloud method: consumers are asked to state, at every step, what they think will happen and why they click specific buttons. If a customer, somewhere in the process, says, 'And now I want to fill out my zip code, but I have no clue where that should go', the designer of the e-commerce platform knows what to improve.

By 'efficiency usability', researchers traditionally mean that if someone wanted to perform a task it should be carried out as

---

* Obviously, estimates on this topic differ between branches and websites. This one is retrieved from: http://seewhy.com/resources/shopping-cart-abandonment.
** There is an ongoing debate about the exact meaning of 'usability'. Effectiveness, Efficiency, and Satisfaction as the drivers of usability are derived from the ISO standards: http://en.wikipedia.org/wiki/Usability#ISO_9241

quickly as possible in as few clicks as possible. If it took 10 clicks to get a book into a digital shopping cart and eventually order it, usability professionals would start looking for shorter routes so the task could be performed more efficiently. Fewer clicks are generally regarded as more effective. This at some point cumulated into a patent held by Amazon for 'one-click buying'. While a smart move by Amazon, this is a bit tricky for other online vendors: they now have to explicitly insert an extra click so as not to violate the patent: such patents in my view hamper the overall efficiency of the web.*

By 'satisfaction' usability, researchers refer to the premise that the user of a website or other interactive product should find the experience fun and enjoyable. The mantra has been that high effectiveness, high efficiency and high satisfaction jointly would be a guarantee of success: tick all the boxes and impact and ultimately effect will come to you. It quickly turned out that effectiveness and efficiency – which are most easily achieved when every website adheres to the exact same rules – often conflict directly with satisfaction. And, we started seeing examples of some online stores hitting satisfaction levels deemed sufficient for a successful site while they were indeed very hard to use. Despite the purchase process taking lots of steps, their visual appeal seems to have helped them achieve a comparatively large effect.

For quite a few years, usability was the domain of usability experts. These experts would 'know' how a product should be made and they looked at the designs of others. Usability testing happened inside laboratories where people were invited to try a new website somewhere in a small room in an office building. This practice seems to be changing. Currently it has become possible to allow for interactive testing while the customer is in the comfort of their own home. We can overlay a number of tasks over a website that we want to evaluate, and we can easily present this overlay to a small number of visitors. Usability studies, once only conducted

---

* In 2006 the patent was challenged and indeed changed for the US. In Europe the patent was never granted.

by experts, is now being carried out by customers through interactive technologies.*

ONLINE TESTING

Online usability testing was derived from an earlier idea that websites themselves could be used directly to test the effect of changes in the design of those websites. Different versions of a website or email provider could be tested without bringing people into the lab. The story about the home draught beer system and the smartphone in the previous Chapter was an example of this idea. The idea of online testing is very popular and is coined 'A/B-testing': we directly compare the effect of versions A and B of our website by showing version A to a number of consumers and logging their response, then showing version B to a number of other consumers.

These tests are sometimes about usability issues: where should I place the PURCHASE NOW button to make sure many people actually click on it? Or where should I put the shopping cart icon so that people can actually find it?

However, since online testing is very inexpensive people started to test everything they could think of– as you browse the web yourself you are likely a participant in hundreds of different tests every day. Marketers would test whether the corners of the BUY NOW button should be rounded or square. They would compare one shade of blue for the background color of the page with another shade of blue: apparently light blue results in slightly more sales.

However, since testing had become so easy and cheap, often the choices of tests would not be informed by any social science theory whatsoever. Testing over the last few years has become largely a-theoretical. This means that nowadays versions of websites that are selected using A/B tests often suffer from the same problems as data-driven recommender systems: since marketers do not know

* A great Amsterdam-based start-up called Usabilla offers exactly this service.

the cause of any differences they find it is very hard to generalize their findings. Hence, while light blue might have worked for some, it likely does not work for others.

Besides the fact that A/B tests are often not very well substantiated theoretically – which is something that keeps surprising me since our common knowledge of the social sciences is tremendous – the current A/B testing craze suffers from other problems. The home draught beer system and the smartphone example already made clear that it is implicitly assumed that the customers that participate in the A/B test are the same as those who visit the website after the test. This might not necessarily be true: the first visitors to visit a new web-service are likely more tech-savvy than late adopters. This means the results of the test might not generalize. The effects might not always be as dramatic as in the home draught beer system example, but it is important to understand exactly what is implicit about the popular online testing methods.

A second problem that I personally have with A/B testing is of a statistical nature: when can a marketer actually meaningfully conclude that version A is better than version B? If we show version A to one customer who decides not to buy the product, and we show version B to the next customer who decides to buy, should we then always select version B? Is one customer sufficient to pinpoint the effect of the two versions? This problem is often even more complicated online since the effect-visitor ratio is often small: what do we do when 6 out of 10,000 customers purchase the product using version A, and 9 out of 10,000 purchase the product when confronted with version B? Some marketers would say that version B is clearly 50% better, but the above numbers are, I hope you agree, not terribly convincing. It is a really tricky question to decide when one should stop the test and choose one of the two versions. This is especially troublesome since in reality no two versions will have the exact same effect: you are offering customers something different, so they are likely to differ in their effect, albeit that the difference might be very small. This means you can keep on testing continuously – if you have enough creativity –

and you will never settle for anything.*

However, obviously testing only versions A and B is insufficient. What if you change the shape of buttons, and the background colors, and let's also test for different font sizes while we are at it. You would not want to compare the buttons first and then the colors, since the colors might interact with the buttons: rounded corners do well on dark blue, while square corners do well on light blue. Welcome to the wonderful world of 'multivariate testing': it is possible to test all different options in one go!**

Multivatiate testing software will ensure that all possible combinations of button corner, background color, and font size will be displayed to customers. If we have 2 colors, 2 corners, and 2 font sizes, this gives us 2 × 2 × 2 = 8 versions of the website to test. However, if the designer is creative and thinks of 4 different font sizes within the button, which are independent of the font size on the page, and four different color borders for the product images, then we are at 2 × 2 × 2 × 4 × 4=128 possibilities. Obviously a computer easily tests this. However the actual interpretations by us humble humans might be tricky.

I believe testing – and multivariate testing – is a very good idea. However, currently the execution is often lousy. I think it's a very good idea to test existing theories in your domain: theories will tell you which variables are likely to have an impact and your tests will show you that some social science theories are wrong in your specific context. However, without any theory the number of

---

* Lots of people are somewhat aware of the concept of 'statistical significance' in which $p(D/H_o)$ – the probability of the observed result (or a more extreme result) given that in reality the effect of the two versions is exactly equal – is computed. When this probability is smaller than 5 percent we often choose to reject the null hypothesis and accept the 'fact' that the effect of the versions is unequal. However, this cut-off is arbitrary, and it does not always lead to a correct choice. For a more elaborate discussion see Kaptein & Robertson, 2012.
** Here I am using 'multivariate' to refer to multiple independent variables. This is often used in practice. However, statisticians do not necessarily use the term multivariate to refer to multiple independent variables, but often refer to multiple dependent variables. Strictly, both uses of the word are appropriate: multivariate simply refers to the study of multiple variables.

comparisons grows very, very fast, and the opportunities to generalize the results decrease quickly. As such, multivariate testing
only worsens the theoretical problems introduced by A/B testing.
And also with multivariate testing it is fairly unclear when to stop
a test: how many customers and how many purchases do I need to
see before deciding that one version is better than the other?

This raises a fairly subtle statistical problem. Many multivariate
and A/B testing software packages will show the marketer a 'statistical significance test'. This test is often interpreted as a number
or indicator that can decide whether the difference that you find (6
out of 10,000 vs. 9 out of 10,000) is real or is due to chance. To do
this the software calculates a p-value: the p-value is the probability
of finding the results you found (or even a more extreme result),
given that in reality the performance of both versions is exactly the
same. (It is thus NOT 'the chance that the results came about by
chance', which is a ridiculous sentence anyway.)

If the p-value, and thus the chance of getting the result that
you got when the two versions perform equally is very small, then
marketers decide that the difference is not due to chance; often
erroneously., Besides being logically wrong, the conclusion is also
too simplistic and of hardly any business relevance. This is not a
statistics book – although we will cover some more stats-topics
later on – but it is good to know for anyone who might ever use
multivariate testing that small p-value will also occur by chance
when there is no real difference: as long as you run enough tests
you will find small p-values every now and then.[*] Unlikely but
possible things eventually do happen. For instance, a series of
twelve consecutive blacks on the roulette table, while extremely
unlikely, have happened and will happen again in the future.[**] Especially with multivariate testing, when you perform lots of tests,
you will occasionally select a 'wrong' version. The results will be

---

[*]   Ok, one more point on significance testing. The procedure can be useful,
but is based on a number of assumptions. If these are violated, than the
results are often meaningless. Also (a bit more technical): $p(D|H_o)$ is not
always equal $p(H_o|D)$.

[**] The probability of this happening given a 'normal' roulette table with 37
numbers of which 18 are black, is $(18/37)^{12} \approx 0.000176$

statistically significant, but still a coincidence. Because of your large number of tests, unlikely results will happen fairly often.

There are many more problems with the typical test used for multivariate testing. In the end, I think it's wise to remember that statistical significance is not equal to real-world significance. Interpreting complex tests is complex, and should not be taken too lightly. Many current multivariate testing approaches only reinforce the marketer, but do not really lead to better business outcomes.

THE DANGER OF CUSTOMER ENGAGEMENT

A/B testing, usability testing, and multivariate testing have all increased the impact of online communication. By constantly testing new ideas and measuring their effects, online stores and services can iteratively increase their impact. However, I firmly believe we can do much better if we start testing in a better way.. We are too often concerned with the background color of an email even if this might not be a prime driver of the behavior of customers. The impact of changes in the background color on human decision behavior is likely limited. In the next chapter we will dig into psychological mechanisms that are meaningful for decision-making so we can truly understand the behavior of customers online. However, first I would like to show why understanding the customer is extremely important.

In 2010 when I was working at Stanford University I met Jerry Lindholm, a Finn who was a visiting scholar at Stanford at the time. Jerry taught me how to play golf, and we discussed our work together. Jerry and I discussed some of the problems he was running into when analyzing a data set.

Jerry had access to anonymous data on 50,000 online poker players. The data described how much each of the players was spending on online poker and how often they participated in the discussion forums and other websites about poker each month. These were data describing the consumption behavior of customers – e.g. how much they were spending on online poker – and their online engagement: the data described how actively consumers were talking about poker on product discussion boards. Jerry initially intended to show, as many had done before him, that increasing engagement would lead to increased spending. Thus, the more you joined online discussion boards about poker, the more likely you were to spend money on poker. This is also a part of the rationale behind brand valuing 'likes' on Facebook: If you like the brand then you actively engage and you are more likely to purchase its products.

Jerry started his data analysis by making a chart setting out the monthly engagement behavior and the monthly consumption on the poker website. He had five years of data, and from the chart the relationship was super clear: as engagement in the service went up, so did the spending. There was a clear link between engagement and consumption, just as Jerry had been expecting!

At that time I knew nothing about online poker:* I had never even played a game online. But I had analyzed data that looked a bit like Jerry's data before. From this earlier attempt I was very aware that results that are very clear when looking at aggregated data, might not hold up at the individual level. That is, the patterns we see for groups of people might not hold up for individuals within that group. Primarily, I was thinking that the pattern that Jerry was looking at was not caused by an actual relationship between engagement and spending on online poker, but was rather an artifact of the increasing popularity of the poker website. Over the course of the 5 years, the total spending and engagement had both increased, as had the number of visitors to the website. My thought was that perhaps the number of visitors had increased, and some had resorted to participating in the online discussion boards (engagement) while others resorted to playing (consumption), but that at the level of the individual customer, there was no relationship between engagements and spending.

Jerry and I analyzed the data at the individual level and found a very different pattern from that described in the literature. We saw that people who played a lot, and spent a lot of money, hardly ever posted anything on the discussion boards. And, those who were

---

* By now I have studied the behavior of poker players in a bit more detail. See for example Lindholm, Parvinen & Kaptein, 2012.

very engaged and talked about poker all the time seemed not to spend anything. In fact, when we started analyzing the effects over time for individuals, we could see that many customers came in and started playing poker straight away. These people consumed the product and made the poker company some money. However, after a while some people would stop playing poker, and would start talking about it. These people were very engaged, but did not bring in any money. Since there was a steady flow of new customers, the average relationship between spending and engagement at the monthly level was consistent, but at the individual level the relationship seemed reversed. Engagement actually had a negative effect on consumption.*

Jerry and I presented these results for the first time in Hawaii during the conference that I referred to at the start of this book. For me this joint research was a very good example of our lack of knowledge about the behavior of online consumers. We think we understand what people are doing online and we have very sound theories:

Theory 1: 'People who are active online and write a lot about the brand feel connected to the brand and will buy more of it.'

This sounds very plausible. However, this theory is not true. The true story is rather:

Alternative Theory 1: 'People who write a lot about the brand seem to meet some of their demands purely by writing and thus the motivation for spending is negated. Those who are engaged consume less.'

If we want to have real impact, we need to understand these psychological processes. We should not only look for 'logical stories',

---

* I think this is an interesting reversal: basically it implies that by engaging (talking about a product) you can fulfill your needs and you refrain from buying the product. Whether a similar pattern holds for products other than poker remains to be seen.

but we should find the data that support these stories. The logical stories are only really useful if they are tested and validated.

SUMMARIZING

In Chapter 3, I said that to be successful online we need to exploit the full reach of the web. I described how you can reach the right customers. In this Chapter I have tried to give a very brief overview of some of the historical efforts to increase impact once these customers arrive at a website. I have described personalization efforts in e-commerce, and have explained, in brief, how some of the personalization algorithms work. If forced to summarize this chapter into a few bullets then this is what they would look like:

- Increasing the number of options and providing lots of choices to consumers does not necessarily increase impact.
- First the choice paradox was attacked using product categories, providing a clear structure to browse the large catalog of online stores. Second, companies started providing search functionality.
- Categorization and especially search options were effective, and certainly increased impact, but had a negative side effect: the limited ability of customers to stumble upon new products. This led to the development of recommender systems.
- Recommender systems personalize the products you see on the basis of the behavior of others, provided that sufficient data are available.
- In addition to recommending products much has been done to improve the usability of online stores. Again, the impact has increased (But this is in fact quite low if the consumer cannot find the BUY NOW button).
- AB tests and multivariate tests gave online marketers the opportunity to try out different versions of their online stores and see which version worked 'best'.
- We do not yet understand everything that happens online. Although one version of a website sometimes performs 'better' than another, we often have no idea why.

5

HOW DOES OUR BRAIN WORK?

The store in which I bought my book for the trip to Hawaii has a corner with a number of small boxes, each of which has a small door with the name of a customer written on it. The store personnel call them 'wish boxes'. They have about 500 of them, one for each consumer: the one in the upper left-hand corner is mine.

That day, as I walk out of the store with the book The Philosopher and the Wolf *by Mark Rowlands and* Justice *by Michael Sandel I also notice a book called* The Greatest Show on Earth *by Richard Dawkins. I own most of the books by Dawkins since I am big fan. However, this one I don't happen own yet. Today the book is on offer. However, I have just bought two books so I am not really in need of a third. So, I don't buy the book but I do put it in my wish box: the next time I visit the store I will easily be able to find the book and purchase it.*

Sorry, as opposed to the rest of this book in which I have tried to be honest and truthful, this was a little lie. I have never seen any physical stores with 'wish boxes'. However, online you can find them anywhere: Amazon has a wish list, and several other stores allow you to virtually store the products that you are interested in. In all cases you can indicate products that you might not buy right now, but intend to buy in the future.

There are good reasons to believe that including wish boxes in the physical store pays off. By making you indicate your product preference, the seller increases the chances of a future purchase.

This holds true regardless of the price-quality trade-off of the product that you are interested in.

In 1966 Jonathan Freedman and Scott Fraser showed how important the effect of commitment – the fact that you indicate that you will do something in the future – is on your consumer behavior. Commitment influences the decisions of people.[*]

Freedman and Fraser went door to door asking people whether or not they would be willing to place a large sign stating: 'Drive Carefully!' in their front yard. The sign was fairly ugly, and hardly anyone thought it was a good idea to place such an ugly sign in their front yard. Only 17% of people actually ended up placing the sign; all others said no.

The number of people willing to place a sign in their front yard, however, increased tremendously when Freedman and Fraser changed their approach. Instead of asking people to place a big sign in their front yard the researchers went door to door to ask a new group of similar people whether or not they were willing to place a small adhesive sticker in their windows. The sticker read 'Drive Carefully!' and almost everyone they asked was willing to do that. The real genius however came two weeks later: the two researchers returned to those houses that had been willing to place the sticker, and asked whether or not they were willing to place the ugly sign in their yard. This was the exact same sign they had tried previously but this time the response was quite different: those people who first committed by placing the small sticker in their windows were now much more likely to accept the sign. A whopping 76% of the total group approached using this second scheme eventually ended up displaying the sign.

The study shows that people who identify themselves with the ultimate goal of the campaign by placing the sticker are much more inclined to actually comply with a larger request in the same vein later on. This is exactly what the wish boxes intend to do: they give the customer an option to quite easily state which products they are interested in. This then increases the chances of a final sale!

---

[*] For the original article see Freedman & Fraser, 1966.

Besides being interesting in its own right, this example also demonstrates that human behavior is not solely driven by a balance between price and quality of the product or the mental gains and losses associated with an action. The cost of placing the ugly sign did not change because the sticker was placed first.

A large number of psychological processes outside the price-quality trade-off influence our decision-making. In the previous chapters we explored how the impact of online communication had increased by reaching out to the right customers and making desired behaviors as easy as possible. Making it easy to find a product, fill out the credit card details, and click the buy-now button increased the effect of online communication. However, as discussed in Chapter 2, the effect is still not nearly as great as we would wish: impact and reach still seem to be inversely related. It seems that we missed something when moving from offline to online. In this chapter I will argue that what we missed is a proper understanding of the psychological foundations of persuasion. Our ability to influence decision-making online is somewhat lacking.

THE USE OF PSYCHOLOGICAL INFLUENCE

Our failure to properly use psychological influence principles has led to the fact that technology-mediated communication, while very impressive in its range, lacks impact. And thus, ultimately, online communication efforts lack effect. In this chapter I will show a number of examples of psychological influence and I will explain why these examples are effective. If you understand human information processing better, you will also be able to better understand why psychological influence is hugely effective.

Let us start out with a little example before digging into the theoretical explanations. The chances are pretty good that in the city or village you live in – or one nearby – there is a cute little museum or historic building that you could visit. The chances are also that you have never visited it. The museum is where the tourists are; it isn't where the locals go. Now suppose that the local newspaper publishes a notice that the museum is about to close. It will be restored, and because of this it will not be open to the public for the next two years. There is only one more week left to visit the museum before it closes down.

Many churches, museums, and other historic buildings which are closing down for restoration have noticed the effect this has: that last week it will be busier than ever. The chances are that you will actually visit the museum yourself, even though it would never have crossed your mind if it wasn't for the notice in the newspaper.

Why does this happen? The museum has not changed, and it was there at your disposal all the time. Also, the ease of visiting the museum has not become any greater. Likely, the ease has actually decreased: you now have to make room in your agenda this week, instead of having the convenience of long term planning. In this example it also seems that the trade-off does not merely concern quality and costs or pleasure gained from the visit,. Apparently, there are other drivers for your behavior.

Rational economic decisions

Theoretically both the decision to place a Drive Safely sign and the decision to visit the the soon-to-close museums are economic decisions: They both question how you divide your time and re-sources between possible actions. It might likely give you some satisfaction* or pride to place the sign, but you will have to trade this off against the mental burden of making your front yard a bit uglier. The decision to display the sign, yes or no, will be a trade-off of the possible pros and cons of the action.

This chapter will deal with the impact of psychology on eco-nomic and other decisions. However, it is important to first think about decisions without the annoying interference of psycholo-gy. Economists historically studied economic decision-making without ascribing any psychological mechanisms to the actors involved. And this provides a useful starting point for thinking about our own decision-making processes.

---

* As we will see in a bit, economists love the word 'Utility' as opposed to satisfaction or happiness etc. However, Utility is often erroneously interpre-ted as a means by which every decision can be rationally interpreted. As far as I understand it, that was never the goal of economists.

Economists were – and still are – interested in consumer decision making: Why did you buy product A and not product B? In essence, this main question is quite aligned with the aim of this book. However, economists started by offering normative* theories describing how people ought to behave in specific decision-making situations. These theories were based on a small number of relatively simple assumptions about people that were all easily captured in mathematical formulae. From these formulae, the economist could derive what people ought to do in specific situations; at least when assuming the starting assumptions were correct.

Economists who study decisions have often done so by presenting people with different, competing, choices. They would present a group of people with such choices and then subsequently study the individual decisions. For example you would be asked to choose between the following two options:

A: You will get 10 USD
B: You have a 50 percent chance of winning $20

The economists themselves, long ago, thought that people would find both choices equally attractive: the value of A is clearly 10 USD. However, the value of B, in the long run, is the same: .5 * 20 = 10 USD. Hence, there should be no difference between the above two choices, and economists thus expected about 50% of the people to give answer A and 50% to give answer B, The choices were equally attractive.

Reality is different, however. If you present a group of people with the above choice, the vast majority of people prefer choice A. Hardly anyone selects B. Hence, people seem not to value both choices equally but rather to prefer option A.

Scholars outside economics started arguing that we needed psychology to understand decisions like this. However, this is not true: the economists came up with a very nifty response that ex-

---

* Normative here means that the theory describes the norm of how to behave. It does not necessarily describe what people actually do.

plains the favoring of A, and actually explains many economic decisions. Economists declared it the idea of 'utility'. Utility is what we all strive for – which is not the same as money, although related. We humans aim to maximize our utility.

Disentangling utility from money makes it very simple to explain the choice of A instead of B. Economists postulated that an increase in money from 0 to 10 Euros gives one more utility than an increase from 1,000 to 1,010 Euros. This is sensible since receiving 10 Euros when you have none allows you to buy food, while if you already have 1,000, the 10 make less of a difference. However, this implies that money and utility do not scale in the same way. This makes it mathematically very simple to demonstrate the superiority of choice A over B. Since the utility does not increase linearly, the expected utility of B is actually lower than that of A. Thus people would favor option A.[*][**]

This sparked the idea of 'utilities' which became the cornerstone of micro economic theory. Economists analyzed different choices in terms of the utilities they had for those involved in the decisions. To do this formally, they had to make a number of assumptions about those making the decisions. These assumptions were necessary so that each possible action could be measured by its utility, and so that it would be clear that whichever action led to the highest utility would be preferred. The core assumptions about utilities are the following:

---

[*] This seems not to be intuitive for everyone, so it might be clearer using a numerical example. Let's say that an increase in money of 10$ (coming from 0) provides us with a single utility point: utility +1. Thus, this is the value of option A. For option B, there is a 50% chance of gaining 0, and a 50% chance of gaining 1 (the step from 0 to 10), +.8 (the step from 10 to 20). The latter step is smaller due to the non-linear relation of money and utility. The expected value of B is .5 * 1.8 = .9 and thus indeed lower than that of A.

[**] OK, one more: my editor asks whether the preference for A is not caused by the fact that people avoid taking risks. Probably that is partly true, but that's a psychological explanation: I was looking for a rational economic explanation.

- Completeness: all possible actions that a human being can perform can be ranked according to their utility.
- Transitivity: if the utility of an option, for example option A, is higher than that of B, and the utility of B is higher than that of C, then A by definition will also have a higher utility than C.

These two simple assumptions regarding utilities are actually everything the economists needed to describe, understand, and predict human decision making. These assumptions jointly describe the Rational Economic Man (REM):* the rational decision-maker that customers ought to be. The decision maker is aware of all possible competing actions, knows their utilities exactly, and chooses whichever action gives the highest utility.

These assumptions, and the normative description of human behavior which can be derived from them, have done no harm to economists: a multitude of Nobel Prizes have been awarded for the analysis of human decisions given the framework of utilities. And, the analysis of decisions using this limited number of assumptions has not only been used in economic science: the utilities involved in decision problems have been used to analyze the outcomes of wars and the actions taken by different countries during the Cold War. The use of the theory of the rational economic man was widespread.

While the theory of REM is fantastic in its simplicity, it leads to a number of counter-intuitive results. For example, the naïve version of the theory predicts that the utility we derive from gaining 10 USD, is the same as the utility that we lose when we lose 10 USD. This however seems not to be the case when we run experiments with actual people: People are inclined to avoid losing as much as possible.** One way to find this out is to ask people how much they need to gain when they are making a bet with a 50%

---

* The Rational Economic Man (REM) is also often called the Econ. See also Hollis, 2007.
** This example is derived from a popular book by Nobel Laureate Daniel Kahneman. For more examples of 'irrational' behavior see: Kahneman, 2011.

chance of losing 100 USD. Apparently, on average, people want the gain to be about 500 USD before this bet becomes interesting. That is far from equally valuing gains and losses.*

THE FIRST BLOWS TO THE THEORY OF RATIONAL DECISIONS
The rational decision theory used by economists to predict (or prescribe) human behavior was quickly criticized by psychologists. The first real blows to the theory however came from a pair of economics researchers named Daniel Kahneman and Amos Tversky. Kahneman and Tversky, in a series of ingenious experiments, showed that often real human behavior did not at all resemble the normative economic theory. Countering some of the original assumptions, Kahneman and Tversky suggested a new theory of rational decision-making called 'prospect theory'. Contrary to earlier accounts, their prospect theory explicitly included a distinction in the utility originating from gains versus losses. In prospect theory, the relationship between monetary value and utility is both non-linear (e.g. the difference from 1 to 11 USD gives more utility than an increase from 1,000 to 1,010 USD, despite the fact that in each case one gains 10 USD) and different from gains as compared to losses. This makes the relationship between money and utility more complex than in the original theory. This new complexity implies, for example, that we attach a special value to products that we already have as opposed to those that we do not have. This additional value is not a property of the product, but rather the result of us valuing losses more heavily than gains. We seem to attach ourselves to the things we have and thus feel losing them is a bigger burden than the pleasure of gaining them. Adding this property, not of products but rather of humans, for the first time introduced psychological processes into the otherwise rational and mathematical theory.

Nonetheless, prospect theory could still be mathematically studied. And hence, contrary to experiments and theories that were suggested by psychologist that did not have clear mathemat-

---

* If people are allowed to make the bet multiple times, this pattern changes.

ical implementation, prospect theory was embraced by econo-mists. However, the psychological experiments went far beyond prospect theory: time and time again so-called economic psy-chologists showed that people did not respond as the economists expected them to. Rather, people seemed surprisingly gullible and they seemed easily influenced by incomplete or inaccurate infor-mation. People would just misinterpret even the simplest infor-mation about products or economic decisions.

While hard to formalize mathematically, the effects of our psychology on our decisions is large. Take the following simple example in which people often err in their interpretation of the situation:

Suppose you have a large pond in your backyard. Unfortunately, algae begin to develop in the pond one day. First you see a small area of algae and then check it out again the next day: the area is about twice as large as it was yesterday. However, it is still a very small proportion of the pond so you are not too worried. You decide that you wait until the pond is about ¼ covered before you take any action. After 30 days the pond is about ¼ covered.

The typical question after reading this story is: 'Approximately how long will it take before the whole pond is covered?' And many people err when answering this question. People will guess at least another 30 days while in reality, if the algae doubles each day, you have only 2 days left before the pond is covered.

The pond with algae is an example of non-linear growth. We often expect things to grow in a linear fashion: 2, 4, 6, 8, 10, 12, etc. However, in nature things often follow a different structure. They grow exponentially: 2, 4, 8, 16, 32, 64. Note that on the first 2 inspections the two sequences look the same, and on the 3rd one the two sequences are not yet very distinct. But from there, the two forms of growth quickly diverge. While exponential growth is common in nature, people in experiments seem to be inclined to expect linear growth. This is the source of error in the pond exam-ple.

These kinds of examples however slowly eroded the idea of

our rational economic man. Psychological processes play a role in human decision making, and even the information processing of people seems to be erroneous quite often. To really explain and predict human behavior, we apparently needed theories distinct from those developed by economists. Psychologist had long studied the strong effects of communication on human decision making. And while most of these studies were not of a formal mathematical nature, they do offer great insight into the processes by which people make decisions. Some of these psychological experiments on information processing prove very useful in understanding some of the not so rational decisions that people make.*

HOW DO PEOPLE PROCESS INFORMATION?

Let's have a closer look at the theories originating from within psychology, as opposed to the formal mathematical theories of human behavior proposed by economists. One of the core ideas, which over the years has emerged many times, is the general idea that there are two distinct ways in which we process information. While a large number of such 'dual processing' models exist, I will try to explain here one of the most famous ones, since the idea of dual processing is one of the core ideas that psychologists added to rational decision-making originated by the economists.** Dual processing models can be used to explain quite a number of deviations from rational theory, and as such are extremely useful.

In 1986 two researchers named Petty and Cacioppo were pioneers of dual processing models with their Elaboration Likelihood Model (ELM). This model attempted to predict what the effects of specific messages would be on human decision making by con-

---

* Both in economics as well as psychology there are heavy debates on the topic of 'rationality'. As this book is written for a larger audience I will often ignore a number of the details of the theories I put forward. The current discussion of rationality is very informal but it tries to capture the main elements of the theory. I apologize to both psychologists and economists for not spelling out all the details.

** The dual processing idea emerged many times. For some examples see: Booth-Butterfield & Welbourne, 2002; E.P. Petty & Cacioppo, 1986; of R.E. Petty & Wegener, 1999.

sidering different ways of processing a message. This is easiest to explain using a simple example: Suppose you are participating in a survey in which you are asked to evaluate your own boss. The survey asks you to state whether or not your boss is a good leader, on a scale of 1 (no not at all), to 10 (yes very much). However, before you are allowed to answer the survey question, you are shown the responses of some of your co-workers. Your co-workers, on average, rate your boss a 9: that's pretty good. Besides the average evaluation, you also get to see a number of the arguments that your co-workers have for this positive evaluation.

According to Petty and Cacioppo, and their famous model, what will happen is the following: You already have an opinion about your boss. That's the starting point. Let's say that your opinion is a 6. Then, before giving your response, you are exposed to a persuasive message: the ratings by others and their arguments might influence your opinion. From the moment you receive the message, two information processing systems kick in: your central processing system and your peripheral processing system. Let's start with the first. Your central processing system, provided it has the time, will scrutinize the content of the communication. What exactly do my co-workers say? And, do I agree? The central system puts all the pieces together and basically functions as the rational decision maker economists once thought we all were.

At the same time, the peripheral system is also active. This second information processing system lacks rationality and rather makes its choices based on 'heuristics': mental short-cuts that allow us to quickly reach conclusions without too much effort. Heuristics are a kind of lazy information processing method: You do not evaluate all the information but rather you take a short-cut. A simple example of such a heuristic is the simple idea that if everybody goes left, then I go left as well. I follow the others without elaboration. These heuristics make our life very easy because they save us the trouble of thinking deeply. Your peripheral information processing system will lead you to the following conclusion: All of my co-workers give my boss a 9, so apparently he's worth a 9. I will save myself the trouble of actually evaluating my boss and just fill out a 9.

While this second system sounds a bit dumb and thoughtless – which it is – it is essentially very useful: Peripheral processing saves us lots of time and effort. And, additionally, the conclusions that our peripheral system draws are often not too bad: if everyone thinks the boss is great, then that might actually be the case. If your co-workers have already applied the heavy mental burden of central processing, then by the time you get the survey and their responses you can save yourself the trouble.

Cialdini, one of the researchers who is very well-known for studying processes of influence, calls the responses by the peripheral system 'click-zoom reactions': Everyone does something (click), so I will do it (zoom). No mental effort, no thinking, just click-zoom. It seems that these kinds of reactions are heavily ingrained in human nature, and it could very well be that it is evolutionarily beneficial to act this way: if you make great decisions with little effort using click-zoom responses this is beneficial for your survival.

The existence of two systems is now recognized by one of the famous creators of prospect theory, the theory that gave the first blows to the theory of rational choice, Daniel Kahneman. In his book *Thinking Fast and Slow,* Kahneman does not call the two systems central and peripheral, but rather talks about System I and System II. Contrary to what you might expect, he calls the rational information processing system, System II, and peripheral processing system, System I. System I thus describes our automated and heuristic information processing. Kahneman also gives an evolutionary explanation for the existence of System I and postulates that System II, our rational or central decision-making system, was added much later than our System I. And with every decision the two systems are both in play: our mind needs to decide whether to follow its click-zoom response, or rather to ponder on the topic and make a well informed decision.

APPLYING THE TWO ROUTES TO PERSUASION

The ELM – the Elaboration Likelihood Model by Petty and Cacioppo – is a little more sophisticated than just the assumption that we have two routes of information processing. Petty and Ca-

cioppo describe clearly all the ways in which a message can influence our attitudes or behaviors. Back to the example: You are
asked to evaluate your boss and you are provided with the opinions of your co-workers and their reasoning. When you first see
this information you are likely to make a rather uninvolved first
decision: will you read it all and tune in your central processing, or
will you go with the crowd? The information that you receive itself
impacts on this first choice: if for example there are 100s of evaluations from co-workers, this is likely too much to read, and you will
be more likely to switch to peripheral processing. Thus, a message
can influence you through one of the two routes of information
processing, but the message itself can also influence which of the
routes you are likely to take.

After you have made your choice regarding your processing
strategy, it still needs to play out. If you agree with the comments
of your peers, then it's likely that both peripheral and central processing actually lead to the same evaluation: You either click-zoom
and mark a 9, or you read the positive reviews, believe them, and
note down a well thought out 9. If both systems lead to different
answers, then it's likely that you respond to System II, provided
that the environment and your personality permit it. If you disa-
gree with the remarks by your colleagues, you might, after elaborate processing, arrive at the 6 mark you had in mind before you
received the additional information. However, if you are too busy,
you are likely to go straight for the click-zoom 9. If the latter is the
case, you are likely to be less certain of your choice than if you had
arrived at the same 9 (or at the 6) using central processing.

Not only does the message influence your tendency to use one
route rather than the other, but the environment will also play a
role. If you have a lot of distractions, or a lot of stress, you are more
likely to use your peripheral processing. If you have to give the survey response within 10 seconds, you simply do not have the time to
use your central processing powers to their fullest.

That last paragraph contained a lot of 'likelys' and 'mights'. That
was deliberate. While the normative decision theory by economists does not permit a likely or a might, and all actions are clear

after the utilities are clear, most descriptive psychological theories
are full of 'ifs' and 'maybes'. The theory of dual processing (e.g.
Peripheral or Central, or System I and System II) sounds like a convincing explanation for the effects of persuasive messages. However, using that theory, we would predict that you either mark your
boss down as a 9 and are uncertain about it (peripheral processing),
mark him down as a certain 9 (central processing and agreement)
or a certain 6. Thus, while the idea of two processing routes is useful in hindsight – once I know that you have provided a 6, I have
sound reasoning for why this happened – the theory is not very
suitable for predictions. This puts us in a situation in which we
have, on one hand, formal mathematical theories of behavior that
are mostly wrong in practice, and on the other hand, psychological theories which seem right after the fact but can hardly be used
for prediction. Hence, the latter theories are hard for us to use if we
want to predict or improve the impact of online communication.

The example of evaluating your boss shows the many outcomes
one could derive from using the ELM. However, there are even
more: researchers have shown that personality plays a large role
in processing, and hence not only will the message itself and the
environment influence the effect of messages, but so will your personality. Adding to that, other researchers have shown that messages that often lead to a click-zoom response can also backfire:
if you feel you are being tricked by the time you get to central
processing, you might respond even more negatively which would
be unfortunate for your boss in this case.

All of these additions make it very hard to determine exactly
what we need to do to improve the impact of our communication.
The prevailing theories about human decision making are not formalized sufficiently to predict the responses of people. However,
we can hardly ignore peripheral processing: clearly we do not behave in a purely rational way, and the effects of peripheral processing can be significant. To understand why we should respect
peripheral processing and embrace it, let's look at how great the
effects actually are.

How great are the effects of peripheral processing?

So, people are not necessarily rational,* and psychological processes play a role in our decisions. The evolutionary development of
System 1 appears to play a large role. Actually, how big is the role of
System 1 in our decision making? And is that role large enough to
begin to explain the lack of impact of interactive media?

Well, let's start again with an example, in which System 1 is in
play:

On some occasion, you end up in a hotel room. Perhaps you are on
a business trip. In any case, you are in your hotel bathroom you see
a sign with the following text:

> *We are trying to save the environment. If you use your towel more
> than once, you will save a significant amount of water and deter-
> gents. This way, you can contribute to a better environment for all
> of us.*

> *The management*

For the sake of convenience we are assuming that you normally do
not reuse your towels, and thus the note asks you to consider starting this habit. The information is likely processed immediately: if
you are busy, it will go through your peripheral system; if you have
more time and motivation, it might go through your central processing system. The peripheral message here is the appeal made by
the 'management'. The management runs the hotel, and thus they
are an ostensible expert on how to behave in hotel rooms. Your
click-zoom response might be: The management knows what is
best, so I will follow. This is fairly similar to the previous example
in which the majority response influenced decision-making via
the peripheral route. On the other hand, there is a clear argument
of environmental damage in the message which you might agree
with when processing centrally.

---

* Again, there is heated debate about what is rational. For a great description see Manski, 2008.

While I would advise you to reuse your towel, the aim here is not to push my personal preferences. The goal was to see the large effects of click-zoom responses: to see how our peripheral system influences our decision. Professor Cialdini took the same message as above, and added explicitly a message that would likely be processed peripherally. The new message became:

We are trying to save the environment. If you use your towel more than once, you will save a significant amount of water and detergents. This way you can contribute to a better environment for all of us. The majority of our visitors reuse their towels.

The management

If you put the initial sign in half of the hotel rooms, and the new sign, which includes the explicit reference to the behavior of others, in the other half of the rooms, you can start counting which message has the greater effect. This is exactly what Professor Cialdini did, and the effect was enormous. Towel re-usage increased by 26% by merely adding an appeal to our peripheral processing system.[*] Mind you, the argument did not change. The information for our rational mind is still the same. So, it is unlikely that this huge increase was caused by our central processing system: the peripheral system is apparently in play for most of the hotel room visitors, and the appeal to what others have done greatly influenced the decisions of visitors.

Effect sizes of this magnitude seem to be the rule rather than exception in investigations into peripheral communication. Understanding this system, which is not included in formal mathematical decision theories, seems to greatly enhance the impact of communication.

If you are not convinced of the importance of peripheral processing in decision-making, consider the following example:

---

[*] For a more elaborate description see: Cialdini, 2005.

We are trying to save the environment. If you use your towel more than once, you will save a significant amount of water and detergents. This way you can contribute to a better environment for all of us. The majority of visitors who have stayed in this room reused their towels.

The management

This difference in wording is very small. And, there is little reason to believe that this additional information will have a big impact on our decisions when processed centrally. However, via the peripheral system this message certainly has an effect. This time it was click-zoom: an increase of 33%.

This increase is likely due to the fact that doing what other people like you do is an even better mental short cut than just doing what other people do. If you accept the evolutionary origin of the argument then it is understandable that following those like you, those in your own group, is an even better decision then just following other people. Hence, the click-zoom response to the last message is even stronger than to the first.

It is clear that the effects of peripheral information processing on our decisions can be very great. Understanding and considering peripheral processing could greatly increase the impact of communication while retaining the newly gained reach. We can show a message to anyone stating: 'all other people have...', thereby easily increasing the impact. Through this mechanism psychological processing clearly influences the effect of an attempt to influence.

FRAMING AND ANCHORING

Since the remainder of this book will primarily detail psychological effects which function – according to the theory – via the peripheral system, it is good to look at some more examples of mental shortcuts. These examples are intended to demonstrate the large impact that psychological processing via the peripheral system can have on our decision making. In each case, the reach is maintained while the impact is increased: thus, psychological processes can greatly improve the overall effect of communication.

I am particularly attracted to this first example because it clearly shows how, in online communication, we can maintain range and increase impact. Say you are asked to choose between two different types of subscriptions for a prominent newspaper, maybe to *The Economist* for example. You are presented with the following choice:

> *Option 1: A subscription to theEconomist.com. You will have online access to all materials published since 1997. You will get all of this for only $60.*

or:

> *Option 2: A subscription to* The Economist *and theEconomist.com. You receive both the print and web editions. You have access to all the materials published online and you will receive the paper edition every week. You get all of this for only $ 125.*

Professor Dan Ariely showed this exact choice to potential readers of *The Economist*, and found that 68% chose the first online option, while 32% chose the second option. No surprising effects of our peripheral processing systems yet. But just look at the second attempt by Dan Ariely in which an additional option was included. You could now choose between:

> *Option 1: A subscription to theEconomist.com. You will have online access to all material published since 1997. You will get all of this for only $60.*

or:

> *Option 2: A subscription to* The Economist *print edition. You receive the weekly paper edition of the Economist. You get all of this for only $ 125.*

or:

Option 3: A subscription to The Economist *and theEconomist. com. You receive both the print and web editions. You have access to all the materials published online and you will receive the paper edition every week. You get all of this for only $ 125.*

And now suddenly we obtain surprising results. If you look at the newly added second option, you – being rational – would think it would not make a difference: you would be stupid to go for this new option since for the same price you can also get option 3. And, this is indeed what happened: nobody chose option 2. But, surprisingly, the added option did tremendously change the choices for options 1 and 3: suddenly, using this new list of options, only 16% of the visitors chose option 1, while 84% chose option 3. Thus, adding a useless option to the list greatly increased the eventual revenue.*

Dan Ariely explains this difference by what is coined a 'framing' effect: when we apply different frames to our propositions this will influence the final decision. For example, our peripheral system might not know what is a good deal, and it will always be looking for simple comparisons to make a quick and relatively informed choice. It seems as if in the first list of options people perceive that they have to pay an additional 65 USD to get the print edition, and that seems too much. In the second list of options the framing is different when people compare options 2 and 3: now suddenly they can get the online version for free on top of the print edition. Apparently this last offer is much more attractive.

There are many studies that show the effects of framing. When you try to influence someone you can actively present his or her peripheral processing system with a simple comparison to frame the offer differently. This is something that influencers – people who are very successful at influencing others – have done for a long time: A good car salesman will never discuss the price of the navigation system before discussing the price of the whole car. Compared to the 24,000 USD of the car, 2,000 USD is only a small

---

* Obviously no one opted for option two. For an accessible description of this study see: Ariely, 2008.

amount. Vice versa however, if we start with a frame of 2,000 USD, both the navigation system and most certainly the car will appear very expensive.

Another shocking effect of peripheral processing, next to framing, is called anchoring. It looks a bit like framing, but it is slightly different in its execution. As stated, our peripheral system looks for easy comparisons. If you are influencing someone, you can actively choose the most likely comparison. Consider the following examples:

> *Today's offer: Heineken beer. Two for the price of one. (Up to 4 crates per customer)*

or:

> *Today's offer: Heineken beer. Two for the price of one. (Up to 8 crates per customer)*

The two offers are very similar. In both case you get to buy one crate of beer, and you get to take one more home for free. Thus, in both cases the rational, centrally processed, message is the exact same. The only difference in the proposition is the alleged maximum.

While hardly anyone ever goes home with 4 crates of beer at once thus making the first proposition sufficient for the large majority of customers, the second proposition feels different. Apparently, with the second proposition, customers believe that it is quite normal to take 8 crates, because why else would the shop impose such a limit. The 8 crates function as an anchor, an active comparison point, for anyone responding to the offer. In the second case, on average, more cases of beer are sold per customer.

One final example I would like to put forward is a study that utterly surprised me the first time I read it. It is both ingenious as well as impressive in its results. The study extends the idea of framing. The study shows that frames work better when people are willing to accept them, while if people reject the framing their central processing will take over, leading to adverse effects. Consider the following: your doorbell is rung, and on the doorstep you find a postcard seller. He says the following:

Would you buy a card? They are 2 dollars.

No psychological influence or explicit use of mental shortcuts here. However, the seller of postcards could also try to actively enforce a frame:

Would you buy a card? They are 2 dollars, that's cheap!

Now, a frame is added to the message. Two dollars for a postcard is now coined cheap. And, if you accept the frame – and thus accept that indeed two dollars is good value for money for the postcard – then you are probably more inclined to buy the card.

This was exactly the situation that a group of researchers compared experimentally. However, the researchers also added a third version:

Would you buy a card? They are 200 dollar cents, which is 2 dollars, and that's cheap!

The researchers showed that most of the cards were sold using this third message.* That might sound a bit odd, but it is actually quite easy to explain given the knowledge we now have about central and peripheral processing. The frame, 'cheap!', will lead to a click-zoom reaction via peripheral processing. However, our central processing is also always in play: if centrally we decide against the frame, two dollars is not really very cheap for a single postcard, we might not accept the offer. The third version of the offer, however, actively distracts our central processing: the remark about the 200 dollar cents is confusing, and puts a mental burden on our central processing system. Because of this, it is less likely to step in when

---

* For a more elaborate description of this somewhat surprising persuasive strategy see Kardes, Fennis, Hirt, Tormala, & Bullington, 2007 or Davis & Knowles, 1999.

the frame is imposed: hence, more people click-zoom to accept the frame when their central processing was disrupted. This influence technique is rightfully called the disrupt-then-reframe technique.

I hope by now you are convinced of the potentially huge effects of psychological influence. Influencing people is not merely about the offer or request: it is largely about how the offer is framed.

PSYCHOLOGICAL INFLUENCE ONLINE

Since our final aim in this book is to understand impact in mediated communication, with a special focus on online influence attempts, it is useful to see whether the above examples of peripheral processing also occur online. The answer obviously is, yes: the action with the beer crates can actually be found online. And the example of The Economist.com was actually investigated online. We can certainly use the peripheral process when thinking about online communication.

Moreover, online the effects are sometimes very large. There are many examples of successful influence attempts online in which rather than the product proposition but the way in which that proposition was pitched, was changed, often leading to significant differences in impact. While initially those selling online focused on being found, and on the usability of their e-commerce site, recently more and more people have been studying the effects of psychological influence online. And rightfully so: the Economist example increased the revenue per 100 customers from 8012 USD to 11444 USD, an increase of over 40 percent!

Actually, the idea that was put forward when we talked about reusing hotel room towels is also heavily used online. This form of psychological influence, where an appeal is made to 'what other people do', is strongly represented online. We do what other people do, and especially if those people are like us. Click, zoom. This is exactly what online social networks exploit: 'Buy this product. Your friends also bought it!' or '80% of our visitors, visitors just like you, clicked this link'.

Some ways of persuading people are even easier online then offline. I have never physically encountered the wish boxes that I started this chapter with. Online, however, they actually do exist, and 'wish lists' increase the number of sales. These wish lists use the strong principle of commitment in online communication – which we discussed when considering the drive-carefully campaign.

However, not all online attempts to influence have been successful. Some frames which sound plausible to the one creating them actually backfire and have the exact opposite effect. Successfully implementing psychological persuasion is often much harder than the above examples would suggest. And this is not only true online: even offline, in controlled psychological experiments, people often fail to replicate the strong effects found by earlier researchers. This is due to the fact that the environment, the person, and the context all play a role and influences both of our processing systems. Persuasion is thus a complex beast.

A great example of an influence attempt backfiring is a well-known campaign once carried out by national parks in the US. The parks had been experiencing problems with visitors taking home 'souvenirs' such as rocks or branches of trees. This was causing great damage to the parks, so the park rangers needed to discourage this behavior. They put up a sign requesting that people not take home anything from the park. Trying to illustrate that this was a very serious problem, they included the number of people that were estimated to take home souvenirs each year.

The park rangers thought this addition would appeal to central processing and make clear that the problem was indeed one to worry about. It would scare people and convince them of the importance of the message. However, the effect was quite the opposite. Visitors would read the sign including the message that many people took 'souvenirs' each year and think something quite different. This was something they had wanted to do themselves, but often felt disinclined to. Now reading that the behavior was common, they felt much less inhibited: 'if everyone takes souvenirs, then why shouldn't I?' Only when the park rangers changed the sign to show the much larger number of people who did not take home souvenirs, did the behavior actually decrease.

This slowly brings us back to the introduction of this chapter.

On one hand we have great formal normative theories of rational decision making which precisely predict what people should do but ignore our psychological makeup. They ignore peripheral processing, and because of this they often err in predicting behavior. On the other hand, we have elaborate psychological theories which are very useful in hindsight for explaining observations but are often too vague to derive predictions from. I mean, suppose we try to influence someone using a positive frame. If the frame is credible the attempt will be successful via both the peripheral as well as the central processing system. However, if the frame is not credible, it could backfire via the central route. It might also be processed only peripherally, in which case it doesn't matter much that it is not credible: click-zoom. If you put people under stress, they are more likely to resort to more peripheral processing but with too much stress they might become overly critical. The results of your attempts to influence might just go in all kinds of directions, depending on the credibility of the frame. It is hard to judge up front the state of the receiver and the processing route that will be used. All these complexities result in the fact that while the psychological theories are appropriate to explain behavior, they are often ill suited to predict behavior.

FURTHER RESEARCH INTO PSYCHOLOGICAL INFLUENCE
This Chapter described a number of reasons why the initial idea of people as rational decision makers fails. Apparently we have two systems, both of which influence our decisions. One of these two, which is in evolutionary terms the elder, seems very susceptible to 'irrational' influence. However, we have only looked at very specific examples of the effects of this second process. And, you might wonder whether possible museum visitors will respond differently from hotel visitors when asked to reuse their towels. Since the situations in which both occur are utterly different, it is likely that the outcomes will be different. These situational and personal effects make the structured study of psychological influence very challenging.

If we want mediated communication or direct computer-human communication to increase the impact, we will need more than just a few little examples. The examples are too specific, and cannot be used one-to-one in online communication. While it is easy to state that '80% of our customers have...', trying to appeal to the successful hotel room example, it is not, by default, clear what the effects will be. We have a vague idea about the mechanisms by which peripheral processing is effective but in practice we have a very hard time accurately predicting the effects of attempts to influence.

In order to apply psychological influence in online communication we will need more than a few examples. We need a structure to relate and compare influence attempts. If we can group distinct attempts and understand why some work and some won't, we can start to understand better how we can exploit peripheral processing in online communication.

In the next Chapter we will examine such a structure: we will examine a categorization of different psychological persuasion principles. While in my view such a categorization should be carried out based on similar effects of attempts to influence – a similar effect on our peripheral system – this is not the case for the categorizations presented in the next Chapter. Sadly, such characterizations do not yet exist. However, the characterization of persuasion principles that we will study in the next chapter will be useful to enhance our understanding of psychological influence.

Summarizing

In this chapter we have discussed a third possible reason for the limited effect of online communication: the lack of impact. While we reach the right people at the right time and they can use our websites, we still need to understand what drives their decisions. Psychological influence is a good starting point in understanding human decision making. In this chapter we discussed the following:

- People don't make decisions just to optimize their utility. Although theories of rational economic human decision making enable us to predict human behavior, these predictions are often inaccurate

- Our peripheral system ensures that people often show click-zoom reactions: reactions that are based on mental shortcuts and heuristics.
- The psychological basis of decisions can be used or exploited by influencers to generate impact.
- Framing, anchoring and commitment are all successful ways of increasing impact which can be used both online as well as offline.*
- To find out how psychological influence works, however, we need to have a structure to categorize influence attempts which we will discuss in the next chapter.

---

* If you are only reading the summaries at the end of each chapter and feel that you are confronted with a lot of terms that you are unfamiliar with, then you may want to read the chapter.

6

THE SIX 'WEAPONS OF PERSUASION'

One of the first things you will encounter if you walk into my favorite bookstore is a table featuring its bestselling books. On the table you will find neat piles of those books that are popular that week. On the right of the bestselling books there is a display table with 'Special Price' novels. These novels are mostly discounted, and often only a few are available. Since I hardly ever read novels, I normally pass this display table without giving it any attention at all.

A bit further in the back there is a display table featuring books selected by the staff of the store. The employees in the store are often of great help in finding rare books, and they seem to know quite a lot about their stock. This means that I often look at the books that are selected by the staff to see if there is anything of interest. If the table features a non-fiction book that I haven't yet come across, and especially if it's discounted, I am often unable to resist the temptation to buy the book. This time however I am already carrying two new books – which is slightly more than I will need for my trip – so I ignore the display tables.

The display tables in the bookstore deserve our attention because in essence they are implementations of psychological influence. The fact that any particular book is a 'bestseller' gives a clear message to our peripheral processing system: this is apparently a choice that others have made. Using peripheral processing, this display table might thus elicit a click-zoom response. The same is true for the other display tables: the staff's recommendations and

the special offers are both implementations of well-known persuasive principles. These persuasive principles could be applied to virtually every product in the store: one could easily swop the books
on the bestseller table with those on the staff's choice table.

In the previous Chapter we discussed the tremendous impact
that psychological influence, or persuasion, can have. I tried to explain how using peripheral processing, persuasion processes take
place. However, the previous Chapter contained only a handful of
examples. In this Chapter I will try to more structurally detail the
different ways in which people can be persuaded by discussing six
distinct persuasion principles. Giving some structure to the numerous influence attempts that one could make is useful because
it facilitates easy recognition and the creation of potentially effective attempts to influence. The main argument for structuring the
diverse ways in which one can be persuaded is that this structure
can aid us in our final goal: that is thinking structurally about
persuasion can help increase our impact. Since persuasion is so
successfully used in human-to-human communication, it is likely that it will also be beneficial for computer-to-human communication. But before you can teach a computer how to influence
humans, you need to first understand and structure the attempts
at influencing that take place between humans. You will need to
explicitly define which words, sentences, and arguments ensure
that an appeal is actually persuasive.

In this Chapter, I will detail six persuasion principles. These six
principles are not new: Professor Cialdini, an absolute authority
in the field of persuasion, introduced them years ago.* Of course,
breaking down attempts to influence into six distinct principles is
not the only type of breakdown that exists. Nevertheless, I believe
the six persuasion principles provide the most useful taxonomy
for our current purpose. In the remainder of this chapter I will
introduce the six principles one by one, and then detail how these
principles – originating from studies of human-to-human persuasion – can be used in computer-to-human communication.

---

* This is just a small sample of the great work of Prof. Cialdini: Cialdini &
Trost, 1998; Cialdini Trost, & Newsom, 1995; Cialdini, 2001; Cialdini, 2005;
Goldstein, Cialdini & Griskevicius, 2008; and Guadagno & Cialdini, 2005.

SIX 'WEAPONS OF PERSUASION'

Professor Cialdini actually began his study of persuasion by looking at good salespeople. For example, he would visit a car dealer and ask for its absolutely most successful sales representative. He would then follow the salesman around and see how he 'played' his customers. When this type of research originally started, many people, especially salesmen, were convinced that the ability to persuade or sell could not be captured by science. It was an instinct.

However, Professor Cialdini was persistent. He would take notes during sales talks and would try to find the commonalities of successful sales attempts. After noticing some patterns, he took what he believed to be the core arguments, sentences, and remarks leading to successful sales attempts back to the laboratory where he studied in detail what their effect had been. He also investigated whether the patterns that he observed had already been studied in psychological literature.

Professor Cialdini would, for example, see that salesmen often gradually built up the decision-making processes that their customers were involved in. During the first encounter with a customer the aim would often not be to sell a car, but simply to make sure that the customer planned a second visit to the store. Only during the second visit would the conversation actually turn to buying a car. And, it seemed like making the small decision to come back for a second appointment made the sale much easier compared to trying to sell directly on first encounter. This gives rise to the idea that people are more likely to do something when they have already made small steps towards the end goal.

This technique of gradually building up decision making was already known in some psychological literature. It is called the 'foot-in-the-door' technique: once the seller has a foot in the door, a 'yes' to a first seemingly small question, then the chance of actually selling the car increases. In 1966 Freedman and Fraser[*] from Stanford University showed the impact that the foot-in-the-door technique could have. The researchers asked people whether or not

---

[*] This work was also discussed in the previous chapter. For the original article, see: Freedman & Fraser, 1966. A more recent discussion can be found in Burger, 1999.

they would be willing to participate in a study in which a researcher visited their home and took a full inventory of their property – a
process that would take about two hours. Fraser and Freedman
found that only 22 percent of the people were willing to have their
houses searched. However, a number of possible participants in
this rather large study were asked a number of fairly short simple
questions prior to being asked permission to search the premises
for two hours, Amongst those people who had already answered
the short simple questions, the willingness to participate in the
large study was much higher: more than 50 percent of the people
were willing to have their houses searched. That's a huge increase
just from properly using the foot-in-the-door technique.

In addition to linking his observations to existing literature,
Professor Cialdini also examined a number of the patterns he observed amongst salesmen in his own studies. This gave him a very
good overview of those persuasive tactics that worked and those
that did not. He summarized what worked into what later became
known as the six 'weapons of influence', or six persuasion principles:

- Reciprocity: People are inclined to return a favor. If I do something for you, even if it's something you never asked for,
  you will be inclined to return the favor.
- Authority: People follow the advice of experts. If a professor
  advises something, one tends to listen.
- Social Proof: People do what other people do. If you know
  that a lot of people buy a particular product, then you will be
  more likely to buy that product.
- Commitment and consistency: people do what they commit
  to in the future. When people write that they will donate to
  a charity – even if they do not really intend to at the time of
  writing – they are more likely to donate the next day.
- Liking: People do things for people they like. You are probably more inclined to help a friend than to help someone you
  despise.
- Scarcity: People value things that are scarce or special. If a
  product is almost out of stock it becomes more appealing.

In the remainder of this chapter I will elaborate on each of these six persuasion principles.

RECIPROCITY

Slightly tired from a long journey, I am at Kyoto airport looking for my connecting flight. Suddenly a small Japanese girl pushes a rose into my hands. She smiles at me and in perfect English tells me the rose is a gift: she needs nothing in return. However, after a short pause she tells me about a charity that she supports, and asks me whether I have some change I could spare. Fifty Yen lighter I walk towards my departure gate.

Out of the corner of my eye I catch another girl handing a rose to another tourist. He also quickly pulls out his wallet and pays up. Hurrying off, he throws it in the garbage only 100 meters from the location where he received it. After all, it is not very easy to take roses through customs.

The above anecdote is a good example of the use of the reciprocity principle. If I do something for you, you do something for me. The rose that I got as a 'gift' ensures that I am more willing to donate to the charity. Walking away without returning the favor would feel uncomfortable. I have just received a gift, and this creates the feeling of indebtedness towards the girl. The quickest way of settling the debt is to donate to her charity. Interestingly, the second girl cheerfully goes to the garbage can, pulls out the rose, and starts looking around for her next victim.

Reciprocity is a well-known principle in social psychology. Psychologists have shown that people are strongly inclined to return favors. It is suspected that we keep a mental account of all our possible debts, and we do not like to have many outstanding ones. The principle is shown to be so strong that even when we receive a favor we never really asked for, we are inclined to return it: exactly what happened to me after receiving the rose.

The effect of reciprocity can be explained using the idea of peripheral – somewhat mindless – processing. Economists who study long-term competitive decisions have shown that reciprocity is an extremely competitive strategy in negotiation situations. In the long term reciprocity pays off. In game theory the principle is known as 'tit for tat': If I help you, you help me, and if I hurt you, you hurt me. The effectiveness of the tit-for-tat principle in everyday life explains why we have evolved to respond to it so strongly.*

Online reciprocity:
The reciprocity principle is already in use in online and other mediated forms of communication. There are many places where you can receive a free informational brochure – often called a 'white paper' – before you are asked to buy a specific product. By being given the brochure, which contains information that you probably could have found easily elsewhere, you are more likely to 'return the favor' and purchase a product.

There are many other ways in which this principle is used. You might receive a free gift card from a company website you never intended to visit. Or, you might receive free shipping on your next order. All of these are attempts to elicit a tit-for-tat response.

AUTHORITY

As early as in 1974, Professor Milgram showed the tremendously large impact authorities can have on the decisions that people make.** Imagine the following: You are walking down the street and an employee of the nearest university approaches you. He is wearing a white lab coat and he is holding a clipboard: no doubt this is a serious scientist. He looks formal and you immediately recognize him as an authority.

He asks you to participate in an important scientific study. You agree, and you follow him to one of the University buildings. You enter a very professional-looking laboratory. In the lab there is a big table with a machine on it with lots of dials and buttons. In front of the machine there is a list of words written on a piece of paper. The researcher tells you that in the room next door there is a man who has memorized the list of words. You cannot see the

---

* One of the (many) interesting research projects on reciprocity in Social Dilemma games is found in: Komorita et al., 1991.
** This study is very well-known and is, amongst other writings, described in Milgram, 1974. More recent discussions on the topic can be found in Nissani, 1990 of Packer, 2008.

man, but you can hear him. Your task will be to check his memory.

Upon closer inspection you see that the main parts of the machine are a dial and a switch. On the dial there is a sequence of increasing numbers: these are increasing voltages. The switch says 'shock'. If you press the button the man in the room next door receives an electric shock, and you are in charge of the severity of the shock.

After the researcher has explained the workings of the machine you are asked to check the man's memory. When the man makes a mistake, the researcher asks you to give him an electric shock: that is an integral part of the experiment. You start with a relatively mild shock. Upon the second mistake, however, the researcher urges you to turn up the voltage a bit and administer a slightly more powerful shock. This time you hear a short scream from the room next door: the shock is clearly felt.

During the course of the experiment the errors accumulate. Slowly but surely you are urged to crank up the voltage. You hear screams of pain. You are in doubt whether you should turn up the dial even more, but the researcher looks you directly in the eyes and states that it is vital for the experiment that you continue.

If you are in any way like the people who actually participated in this experiment – people randomly selected from the streets by Professor Milgram – then it is fairly likely that you will continue up to the point when the screaming stops, and the man in the room next door goes totally silent. You have ostensibly just administered a fatal shock.*

The results of this study, in which nearly 65 percent of the participants went as far as to kill another human being for not memorizing a list of words, shocked the world (no pun intended!). Of course, the experiment was a fake: nobody was really killed. The screams were faked. But still, many people who participated bought into the cover story. Many of them were severely distressed after participating in the study: they themselves had never expect-

* The study by Milgram was one of the studies that started the discussion on research ethics in psychology. Nowadays it probably would have a hard time getting approval from the ethical committee.

ed they would be capable of such a brutal act.

The most interesting finding of this study however came only later. When other researchers tried to replicate the experiment, they found that if the researcher was not wearing a white lab-coat or if the study was not done at a University, people would stop much earlier. If you removed the signs of authority, hardly anyone was willing to administer the fatal shock.

The study shows the surprisingly large impact of authorities. Like many others, you are likely to be strongly influenced by the opinions of experts and authorities.* Follow up research even showed that if the arguments brought forward by an expert are very weak, that our peripheral system exhibits a click-zoom response and follows, seemingly without thinking. That is the power of authority.

Online authority:

Authority arguments have already been discovered by those who are trying to persuade you online. Online stores will show you the special selection of products their very experienced employees have made. And, they will display authoritative expert reviews of products: musicians recommending music albums, authors recommending books, and actors recommending the newest films.

Over the last few years we have also seen an increase in would be authorities in one of the corners of a website: there might be a little man or woman wearing a business suit. You can chat with this fictitious persons and directly ask your own personal questions. An appeal to authority is being made in this situation, too: you see the man wearing the business suit, and click-zoom, you accept the answer.

SOCIAL PROOF

In 1964 a woman was stabbed in broad daylight on the streets of New York. Prior to the stabbing there was a heated discussion be-

---

* An interesting aspect of this study which is overlooked by many is that about 1/3 of the people that participated resisted the expert advice. We will discuss this in more detail in Chapter 8.

tween the perpetrator and the victim, and it is likely that even during the stabbing itself a lot of noise was made.

The fatal incident took place in a busy narrow street lined with high-rise apartment buildings. And it is likely that everyone who was at home at that time heard the fight escalate at least. Many of the residents might have actually seen the terrible incident unfold by simply glancing out of their windows. This was confirmed by subsequent investigation: many of the residents had indeed seen the incident happen. However, no one intervened.*

This incident intrigued social psychologist for years: why did none of the residents help the poor woman? All the spectators declared that they found the incident terrible and unjust, but nobody had stood up.

The rather shocking observation that, even in fairly public situations, spectators do not often aid victims is coined as the 'bystander effect'. The explanation for the phenomenon is the following: people tend to do what others do, especially in new and stressful situations in which they are uncertain; they look around and see what others are doing. And in doing so, they will see that others are also pausing and looking around: they are engaged in the exact same process of deciding on the correct response as you are. Because you see everyone else looking around, you will come to believe that standing still and looking at others is indeed the appropriate response. The same holds for the rest of the audience. During the stabbing in broad daylight – likely a novel and stressful situation – this is just what happened. When someone is assaulted the apparently appropriate response is to stand still and look around: that's what everyone is doing.

In later years social psychologist clearly showed experimentally that this effect is real: we indeed look at what others do to determine our own actions. This principle is called the 'social proof principle'. Social proof leads to the counter-intuitive finding that if you are ever assaulted on the street – or have a heart attack – you are more likely to receive help when there is only one bystander than when there are many.

---

* This incident is described in Cialdini, 2001.

Besides the bystander effect, many other demonstrations of the power of social proof exist. I am personally very impressed by what came to be known as the 'Asch-experiment'.* In the late fifties Professor Asch asked a number of people to perform a number of simple tasks. For example, participants in the study had to compare the lengths of lines drawn on a piece of paper. One piece of paper contained a single line, while a second piece of paper contained three lines marked A, B, and C. It was up to the participant to state which of the lines (A, B, or C) was as long as the line on the other piece of paper.

This task is tremendously simple, and in the initial study only one in thirty five people made a mistake. However, by only slightly changing the setup of the experiment, Professor Asch was able to get more than 75 percent of the people to give an erroneous answer.

The change was pretty simple. Professor Asch contracted seven actors to give their answer to the simple puzzle publicly. All seven actors gave the wrong answer: they would all say 'A', despite the fact that line 'B' was equally as long as the line on the other card. Afterwards, the real participant in the study was then asked to give their answer. Although knowing that it was wrong, what happened often was that after the seven actors said A, the participant would also respond 'A' just to follow the herd.

The effectiveness of social proof is easily explained. In the past, doing what others do would be, and in many situations still is, a very good idea. For example, if you enter a building and everyone is running out, then it is likely that they have a good reason. You can walk in and figure out for yourself that the building is indeed on fire, or you can follow the herd and make a good snap decision. Because following others very often allows us to make good decisions with limited effort, it has become engrained into our system of peripheral processing.

---

* The 'Asch' experiment is described in Asch, 1955 and Asch 1956. However, many interesting videos of the experiment (and replications thereof) can be found online.

Online social proof:
The applications of social proof in online communication are everywhere: many products are accompanied by reviews from other customers, or a series of 'stars' or 'likes'. You might be confronted with the message that 20,038 people have already bought the product that you are looking at, and that twelve of your dearest friends are fans of the brand. In all of these cases an appeal to social proof is made: you should do as the others did and buy the product.

COMMITMENT AND CONSISTENCY

The fourth persuasion principle that I would like to discuss in this chapter is the principle of commitment and consistency: People do what they say or write they will. The foot-in-the-door technique that I introduced at the beginning of this chapter is an example of the commitment and consistency principle: once people say yes to a small request, it becomes more likely that they will also say yes to a large request: people try to be consistent with their previous actions.

Pallak, Cook, and Sullivan* presented a very good example of the commitment principle in a study carried out in 1980. They tried out different ways in which they could motivate people to reduce their household energy consumption. During the study, one group of participants received a number of practical tips on how to reduce their energy usage and then their actual energy usage was measured. A second group received the exact same tips after which their energy consumption was also measured. The only difference was that the second group's participation in the study was publicly announced in the local newspaper. These people were all clearly named and it was written that they were trying to reduce their energy consumption.

Within a month the results of the study became clear. The group of people whose names had been publicly announced consumed much less energy than those who participated in the study privately. The fact that participants had publicly committed to

---

* See: Pallak, Cook & Sullivan, 1980.

saving energy apparently motivated them to reduce their energy consumption.

The power of this principle is often explained using the theory of cognitive dissonance as presented by Festinger.* In this classical psychological theory it is assumed that people greatly value internal consistency: we want our thoughts and actions to correspond. If this is not the case, if our thinking is not in line with our actions, this causes stress or 'dissonance'. The theory asserts that people will go to great lengths to reduce such dissonance: they will change either their behavior or their thinking. In the case of the public announcement in the newspaper, people had to change their behavior to be consistent with the publicly announced goals.

The peripheral system is also important for this principle: In addition to the fact that we ourselves like to be consistent we also seem evolutionarily trained to value consistency in others. If others are consistent then we can trust them and work with them. The consistency principle is a powerful influencer, despite the fact that often it might be a good idea not to stick to not-so-smart promises.

Online commitment and consistency:
Although this principle has long been known, and the effects may be very great, it is still not widely used to increase impact online. There are a few notable exceptions: Amazon.com has a 'wish list' – the example that I used at the start of the previous Chapter. This wish list is actually an attempt to influence employing the commitment and consistency principle: once you as a customer indicate that you will buy a product in the future, you are more likely to actually do so.

LIKING
People tend to do things for people they like. This principle is intuitively quite plausible: you are probably more willing to help out a good friend than to help out a total stranger. Professor Cialdini noticed that good car salesmen actually try to become 'friends' with their customers as quickly as possible. The more the customer

---

* See (e.g.): Festinger, 1957.

liked the salesman, the more likely it was that the car got sold. Terms such as 'liking', 'friend', and so on are all rather vague. You probably would appreciate seeing a bit more evidence for this principle than just a little gut-feeling anecdote. Also, you might be interested to know exactly how you can increase liking and subsequently increase your impact.

One of the ways in which you can increase liking is by increasing similarity. It has long been known in psychology that people who are similar often like each other. For example, if I ask you to fill out a personality questionnaire and then show you the answers given by someone else, you will generally like that person more when their answers are similar to yours.

And it is not just the personality that seems to influence liking. If we share the same hobbies, backgrounds, or even age, we find each other more likeable. This effect is so strong that in the seventies people viewed the 'similarity attraction effect' as one of the few laws of the social sciences.*

Once you know that liking can be created by appealing to similarity you can start showing the effect of the principle of liking. Do people really buy more cars if the seller shares a number of characteristics with them? For example, if they both go skiing in winter, does this increase sales? You might by now recognize that over the last few years you have bumped into a surprising number of salesmen that shared your hobbies and interests: that is just good selling.

Hornstein, Fisch and Homes carried out the most beautiful experiment that I know of which demonstrates the effect of liking using similarity. In 1968 these three researchers intentionally dropped wallets on the streets of New York. They dropped a wallet and waited to see whether it was returned to the lost and found.**

To test the effect of liking the researchers did the following: in

---

* The idea that similarity leads to liking is coined the 'similarity attraction effect' (SAE). Many researchers have studied this effect. Berger (1975) is one of the researchers who named it one of the 'laws' of social science.
** In total they lost their wallet 105 times. The original reference is: Hornstein, Fisch and Holmes, 1968. A more recent discussion can be found in Garner, 2005.

half of the wallets they lost there was a card – resembling a driver's license – that contained an American name. In the other half of the wallets they dropped they inserted a similar card, but this time with a foreign sounding name. The idea was simple: it was likely that an American would find the wallet, and thus that the American sounding name on the card was similar to their own. This similarity increases liking and thus increases our willingness to help. If this were true, more wallets with American sounding names ought to be returned to the lost and found than those with foreign names. And this was exactly the outcome of the experiment. The researchers thus demonstrated that it is not just intuitive that we are more willing to do things for people we like

Like all principles, the principle of liking is also easily explained by considering peripheral processing. Our preference for people that we like – and people that are similar to us – has a clear evolutionary origin. The more someone was similar, the more likely it was that we would be relatives. And, if we were related we would share the same genes. Similarity often confirmed some direct relationship, and to promote our own genes we would be more likely to help a distal family member than someone from a competing tribe. So we can hardly resist requests by our closest family. And, if someone who tries to persuade you is similar or likeable enough, you will click-zoom and comply with the request.

Online liking:
Although the principle of liking is extremely popular in human-to-human persuasion – from salesmen to politicians, they all try to be liked. It is one of the hardest principles to implement in computer-mediated communication. A small number of websites exist that clearly distinguish themselves from others by using an amicable writing style, but whether this truly implements the principle of liking remains to be seen.

I believe that the principle of liking is rarely implemented because many people are unaware of the findings of Professors Reeves and Nass in their book *The Media Equation*. Many people simply do not know that humans respond in a similar way to computers as they do to other humans. Despite the fact that Reeves and Nass showed convincingly that it is true that people can even become 'team members' with computers if we just match the color of the computer screen to the color of a t-shirt. It remains a fact that is largely met with skepticism. If we however accepted these findings, I believe we could use the liking principle much more in mediated communication.

Lately the liking principle has been used in computer-human communication, but via a proxy: social networks rely heavily on showing you the behavior of people that you like. This is not just an instance of social proof: social networks are trying to make attempts to influence even more successful by using the people that you like. You are likely to share similarities with your social network friends, and thus their behavior is going to influence you more than that of random others. While this is distinct from the appeal for similarity that offline salesmen often use, it seems to be a powerful use of the general principle.

SCARCITY

The principle of scarcity states that people assign value to things that are special or rare. In Chapter 5, I gave the example of the museum in your town that was about to close: you've never really felt the need to visit the museum but if you suddenly find out that this is your last chance you feel more compelled to visit.

That example was just an anecdote, but just like the other principles the principle of scarcity has been overwhelmingly demonstrated in experimental studies. The simplest demonstration was the following: Verhallen and Robben[*] asked a number of people to state their 'willingness to buy' a specific product. Half the people in the experiment were asked to rate their willingness to pay for a specific book, while the other half were confronted with the exact same book and with the additional message that the book had 'limited availability'. This minor change in the way in which the products were described between the two groups had a considerable effect on people's willingness to pay: in the second group – the limited availability group – people were willing to pay more for the exact same book.

---

[*] See Verhallen & Robben, 1994.

This finding is somewhat surprising since it is unclear what 'limited availability' even means. Does that mean there is only one copy left? Or are there a few thousand left, which is still a limit but not a very urgent one. To me however this lack of clarity further supports the scarcity principle: it is not about the actual scarcity of the product: your peripheral system will exhibit a click-zoom response in the presence of perceived scarcity and will comply. The study clearly shows that the anecdote of the museum is indeed easily formalized into a proper scientific experiment.

There are numerous explanations for the effect of the scarcity principle. Some theorists believe that scarcity arguments are really just social proof arguments in disguise: if something is almost sold out, then many other people must have bought it. So, if I do what others do I should buy it as well. This, in my view, is much too complicated for a click-zoom response. And neither does this explanation really explain why we suddenly feel the urge to visit a museum that is about to close: this does not tell us anything about what others have done.

Others have explained the impact of scarcity using the central idea that people have an urge to be unique or special. People want to be unique on one hand, but paradoxically fit in with the group at the same time. Although this explanation is complex, the need to be unique does provide a plausible mechanism for the effect of scarcity. If we have a desire for self-fulfillment and uniqueness, it is likely that things that are scarce also appeal to us. Whatever the underlying mechanism, scarcity appeals can greatly improve the impact of communication.

Online scarcity:

Scarcity is also used in mediated communication to increase impact. I think the best example of the use of scarcity online is provided by Booking.com: This online service sells hotel rooms and often show that there are only 2 rooms left, while 3 people are currently looking at the room: that's scarce.

Scarcity has played a role in the success stories of many Internet companies. When Facebook started as a social network, MySpace and Friendster already existed and were by far larger than Facebook. Technically MySpace and Friendster were no worse than Facebook. However, Facebook had the power of scarcity: Initially you could only get a Facebook account if you had a @harvard.edu email address. This was slowly relaxed to include @yale.edu, @stanford.edu, @berkeley.edu, etc. etc. It was clear that Facebook was not for everyone: Facebook was kept artificially rare. This market-entry strategy is most likely what made Facebook grow beyond MySpace and Friendster, and eventually become the largest social network in the world.

WHERE DOES THIS TAKE US?

The six persuasive principles introduced by Professor Cialdini: Social Proof, Reciprocity, Scarcity, Authority, Liking, and Commitment and Consistency, provide us with a structure to think about attempts to influence. We can now assign specific influence attempts to six distinct principles which are successful via peripheral processing. These six principles are an obvious next step to increase the impact of online communication.

Although some of these principles, such as the social proof principle, are already in wide use in online communication, it is likely that properly implementing these persuasion principles can further increase the impact of online communication. Consequently, persuasion principles can likely increase the overall effect of computer-to-human communication.

Despite the success of specific implementations* of persuasive principles, it has been notoriously hard to predict the effect of an attempt to influence. Although there are many studies that clearly demonstrate that persuasion principles work – at least for large groups of people – it is not always clear in advance what specific implementation of a persuasion principle needs to be used to maximize the impact. One principle can be implemented in many ways, using different images, different sentences, etc., and it is

---

* I am using the word 'implementation' to refer to a specific instance of the principle. For example, one could implement Social Proof in e-commerce by stating that a product is 'popular', a 'bestseller', or a 'top selling product'. The latter three [but there are only 3, so what are the former 3?] are distinct implementations of the Social Proof principle.

often unclear which implementation will eventually be successful. Even though all of the principles seem to have a strong evolutionary basis that makes them effective, there are still situations in which implementations of persuasion principles fail to persuade people. The research work by Cialdini is not informative enough to properly predict which implementation will be successful for a specific person in a specific context.

Professor Cialdini seems to have based his taxonomy of six persuasion principles on similarities between implementations. He grouped together a large body of social psychological research. However, the taxonomy is not directly based on the impact of distinct implementations: it is not the case that every implementation of scarcity will be equally impactful. The principles presented by Cialdini are therefore primarily useful in a descriptive manner: the taxonomy helps you to remember, recognize, and create new attempts to influence but it does not guarantee the success of an influence attempt.

However, if you find the right implementation, the principles of persuasion can greatly increase the impact of communication. Professor Milgram shocked the world by demonstrating that authority arguments can persuade people to kill other innocent people for not memorizing a list of words. Pallak, Cook, and Sullivan showed that a small question followed by a larger question can more than double the number of people who eventually say 'yes' to the larger question. Persuasion principles can thus be of huge importance when we try to create impact.

The persuasion principles are a great next step to increase the impact of mediated communication. The taxonomy presented by Cialdini allows us to categorize attempts to influence, recognize them, and create novel implementations. However, if we truly want impact, we need to be able to determine which implementations work, when they work, and for whom they work. We need a bit more than just a taxonomy and a number of experiments to truly use the persuasion principles as 'weapons of influence'.

SUMMARIZING

In the previous chapter, it became clear that psychological influence can have a considerable effect on human decision making. In this Chapter, I detailed the six persuasion principles as identified by Professor Cialdini. We can now use this taxonomy in our further discussion of impact in online communication. The six persuasion principles bring us one step closer to effective online communication. The principles are:

- Reciprocity: People are inclined to return a favor
- Authority: People often follow the advice of experts.
- Social Proof: People do what other people do.
- Commitment and consistency: People do what they say or write that they will.
- Liking: People do things for people they like.
- Scarcity: People value things that are scarce.

7

MORE IS LESS

Let's return to my favorite bookstore. I am wandering around and take a look at the display table that shows the 'staff's choice'. I notice a book called The Emperor's New Mind *by Sir Roger Penrose. I have greatly enjoyed reading books by Penrose, but this is a title I have not yet come across. So, it sparks my interest. While flipping through the pages of the book I notice that it is filled with formulas so I decide not to buy it for holiday reading.*

Walking out of the store I notice another display table which reads 'special price'. This table also contains Penrose's book. So, the book is both recommended by the staff and currently on sale. While this sounds like an attractive combination, I have made up my mind: I am not buying Penrose right this second.

Walking to the exit I again notice, in my periphery, the book by Penrose. This time however the book is on the display table that reads 'Bestsellers'. So, The Emperor's New Mind *is apparently recommended by the staff, is a bestseller, and is on special offer…*

Although all of these arguments could well be true simultaneously, the combination does strike me as odd. And I am still not very fond of bestsellers: I try to avoid those books that everyone seems to read. So, that argument does not appeal to me, despite the fact that the staff's choice and the special discount are both arguments that could motivate me. I start to wonder whether this stacking of sales arguments is happening for a number of books. I take out my phone and take a picture of the bestseller table, then walk back to take pictures of the 'special price' and the staff's choice tables. As it turns out, quite a number of books are featured on all three of the display tables…

My experience in the bookstore raises a new question about the use of persuasion principles: we now have our list of strategies, or principles as coined by Prof. Cialdini, but we have no clue how best to use these. The research reviewed in the previous chapter showed again and again that using persuasion principles was more effective than not using such principles. So, when a book is recommended by the staff, it on average sells better than a book that isn't. However, we currently do not know whether we should use all the principles we can think of together. Do the effects add up? Or do some principles go together better than others?

The manager of the bookstore seems to know the answer to this question: just make sure you use all the strategies you can think of. And the bookstore manager is not the only one who thinks this way: pick up the average self-help book and you will find a bestseller sticker on the front, a special price sticker on the back, and a number of endorsements by well-known authors stating that the book is the absolute best. According to current practice we should thus stack up all the principles that we know to be as effective as possible. In this chapter we will discuss whether or not this current practice is actually correct.

STACKING PERSUASION PRINCIPLES

The question itself is not really surprising: should we use all the persuasion principles we can think of when we try to influence others? Or, rather, should we pick and choose our principles?

In 2009 I began examining this question. Initially, given the almost trivial nature of the questions and the gigantic amount of social scientific work on how people influence each other, I was expecting to find the answer readily in the literature. Despite the obvious added practical value of a proper answer to the question, I was unable to find any empirical studies. It seemed that no one had compared the use of multiple persuasion principles with the choice of a single principle.

Shortly after I started my search I had the honor to meet with Professor Cialdini at a conference at which he was a keynote speaker. Since the stacking of persuasion principles was at the forefront of my mind at the time, I asked Professor Cialdini how he felt about it. He replied that this was a question he had recently started studying with his team, but he had no answer yet. The work wasn't yet complete nor was it published. So, even Prof. Cialdini, who is an absolute authority on persuasion, seemed unable at the time to give a decisive answer to the important practical question of stacking persuasion principles.

During the period of my search I often talked to Jerry Lindholm about our joint work on Poker Playing (see Chapter 4). Besides being interested in Poker I found out that Jerry was also interested in so-called 'Sales Influence Tactics' or SITs.* In the marketing and sales literature, SITs was the name that sellers used to identify tactics – or tricks – that would help you sell products. Basically, SITs help salesmen to influence their customers. Jerry had just recently stumbled upon the six persuasion principles identified by Cialdini, and noticed that these looked very similar to a number of SITs in the marketing literature. It looked like the SITs Jerry was studying could easily be summarized into the six persuasion principles.

After listening to Jerry explaining SITs as they were used in the sales and marketing literature, I asked him whether he knew of any papers that discussed the use of multiple SITs simultaneously to sell a product: perhaps my rather obvious question had actually been studied under a different name. And, to my surprise, Jerry was able to point me to two studies that directly compared the use of multiple SITs to a single SIT.

The first study that Jerry introduced me to was carried out by Professors Bruce Barry and Debra Shapiro.** And, it had been carried out as early as 1992! Their study set-up was relatively simple: they performed an experiment in which participants were asked to defer an appointment that they had previously made. Half of the participants were shown only one SIT to persuade them to defer

---

* In science it is surprisingly common for the same phenomenon to be studied in different fields using different names.
** The terms in the original article differ from the ones I use here: I am trying to work back from SITs to persuasion principles. For the original study see: Barry & Shapiro, 1992.

the appointment. This group was shown an authority argument. The other half of the participants were confronted with multiple arguments. For this second group both the authority as well as the liking strategies were used. The study clearly showed that the attempts to influence that used a single SIT were more effective than those that used multiple SITs. So, the first empirical study that I found on the topic actually confirmed the initial feeling that I had had in the bookstore.

The second study that Jerry advised me to look up was much more recent. It was a study done in 2008 by Professors Cecilia Falbe and Gary Yukl.* They also studied SITs instead of persuasion principles, and the categories that they used differed from those used by Prof. Cialdini. However, Falbe and Yukl did study exactly the question I was interested in: are multiple principles more effective than a single principle? Falbe and Yukl studied the use of SITs in a different context from Barry and Shapiro. They studied the use of SITs by managers and the impact this use had on their employees. Contrary to that previous study, they found that managers who used multiple SITs were often more effective in convincing their employees than those who used only a single SIT. The study showed that during a conversation those managers who stacked SITs were more effective than those who did not.

These studies confused me. First, I was still surprised by having to leave the psychology and influence literature and dig into the literature on sales influence tactics to find any work regarding my question. Second, the two works that I did find had contradictory results. The first study confirmed my own gut feeling, while the second proved me wrong. Nonetheless, I was inclined to follow the first result – not only because it corresponded to my gut feeling. The study by Barry and Shapiro was experimental: they themselves manipulated the number of SITs that were used. This was not true for the study by Falbe and Yukl: Falbe and Yukl studied the behavior of managers in the wild, without any intervention. This approach makes it harder to understand exactly what caused the difference: perhaps those managers that were inclined to use

---

* See: Falbe & Yukl, 2008.

multiple SITs were also friendlier or otherwise more appreciated. Maybe this caused their success, rather than the use of the SITs. Also, the multiple SITs might have been used to support different arguments, which mean that the Falbe and Yukl study answers a different question from my own. I wanted to know whether one should use one or multiple SITs in order to promote a single behavior.

So, I was still pretty much stuck with the same question.

A MULTIPLE-PRINCIPLE EXPERIMENT

I was unable to find a decisive answer to my question. The simple question whether or not a book should be featured both as a bestseller as well as the staff's pick, rather than just one of those headings remained unsolved. So, I had to carry out the experiments myself to answer this question. I decided I would set up a series of experiments to test whether the use of a single persuasion principle was more effective than the use of multiple principles. With the help of Professor Clifford Nass, who I was working with at Stanford University, I designed the following experiment:

You, the participant, enter a room in the University and are asked to take your place behind a computer. You know that you are participating in an experiment, and you will need to perform a number of tasks on the computer. The first task is simple. You are asked to imagine the following:

> *You have just survived the crash of a small plane. Both the pilot and co-pilot were killed in the crash. It is mid January, and you are in Northern Canada. The daily temperature is 25 below zero, and the night time temperature is 40 below. There is snow on the ground, and the countryside is wooded with several creeks crisscrossing the area. The nearest town is 20 miles away. You are dressed in city clothes appropriate for a business meeting. You manage to salvage twelve items that you can use to try to survive.*

After you have imagined the somewhat peculiar situation, you are presented with a list of twelve items:

- A piece of agricultural plastic
- A lighter
- A compass
- Milk powder
- Duct Tape
- An extra T-shirt and shorts
- A hand ax
- Iodine Tablets (to disinfect water)
- A gun
- An alarm whistle
- A box of matches
- A map of the area

You are then asked to rank each of the items in their order of importance for your survival. You can drag and drop the most important item at the top of the list, and subsequently drop all the items in their places.

After you have specified your preferred order by dragging and dropping, the following message appears on your screen:

Some of the answers you gave were correct, but some answers can be improved. You now have the opportunity to improve your answers

In reality, there are no wrong answers. In reality, if you submit this list to the best survival experts, they will have difficulty reaching an agreement about the order of the list. This is what made the list a good tool for our research: since there was no true best answer, we could try to influence your preferred order using persuasion principles. To test our initial question, we split the participants up into three groups. The first group would get a number of suggestions to move items in the list up or down. These suggestions were ostensibly based on the behavior of previous participants in the study. The second group also received tips on which items to move up or down, but this time the suggestions ostensibly originated from a survival expert. Finally, the last group of three received tips that originated from both the survival expert and the group of fellow participants whose answers agreed. So, we had set up an experiment by which we could directly study the effect of social proof (the other participants), authority (the survival expert) or the use of both of these principles simultaneously.

All the participants received the exact same suggestions for changing their lists. Ensuring our results were only dependent on the source of the suggestions, and not the suggestions themselves. The suggestions were:

> *The survival expert OR previous participants suggest moving the Hand ax [OR lighter, or matches,… or whatever the participant had put in position 7] from position 7 to position 1.*

Since there were no absolutely correct answers, we could directly study whether the Social Proof principle (group 1) had a larger effect than the Authority principle (group 2), or whether the stacking of principles was most successful (group 3).

We suggested 6 of these types of changes to the list. And for each suggested change we would see to what extent the participants complied: If you moved whatever you had at 7 indeed to position one, you earned 7 − 1 = 6 points. If you moved the item up, but not all the way to 1 your compliance score would be lower. If you moved whatever object you had at position 7 to position 4 based on the above suggestion you would obtain a compliance score of 7 − 4 = 3.

THE RESULTS

Once we had enough participants in the study, Professor Nass and I took a good look at the results. The first thing we looked at was whether or not we were able to influence the opinions of participants using the suggestions. We found that every participant in the study had a compliance score that was higher than zero: this indicated that we had managed to change the opinion of our participants in each of the experimental groups. Social proof changed the opinions of participants, authority arguments changed the opinions of participants, and finally using both of these together changed the opinions of participants. However, this should come as no surprise: in the previous chapter we reviewed overwhelming evidence that persuasion principles indeed are effective to influence people's attitudes and behaviors.

What was much more interesting was the comparison between the first two experimental groups and the third group: this was a comparison between the number of principles. So, we started looking at the individual groups. Strikingly, the compliance score in group 2, where the authority principle was used, was almost twice as high as the compliance score in group 1. Thus, we found that in this specific situation the authority principle was much more effective than the social proof argument. The compliance in group 3 was slightly higher than the compliance in group 1 but it was much lower than the compliance in group 2. So, we found that using multiple persuasion principles was less effective than using a single principle: the authority principle outperformed the combination of both the authority and the social proof principles. At last I had my first evidence that, indeed, stacking persuasion principles was less effective than using a single principle!*

Convincing evidence?

A student of Professor Clifford Nass' named Steven Duplinsky had helped me carry out the study. Steven was an amazingly smart Stanford student, and jointly we wrote up our results and presented them at a scientific conference in Canada. We thought we had a great insight to share: multiple persuasion principles are less effective than a single persuasion principle This meant the current practice of stacking all the principles might be wrong.

However, after Steven and I presented our work, the audience seemed much less excited. It was not convinced at all. Basically the consensus was: 'It is clear that in a survival situation such as our experiment people value authorities more than their peers. Actually, people seem to disregard the opinion of their peers in this situation. And, only when a principle is really ineffective – like the

---

* I carried out this experiment together with Clifford Nass, Steven Duplinsky and Estella Marie Go at Stanford University. It can be found in: Kaptein, Duplinsky, 2012.

social proof used in this study – will you find the result that stacking does not work. If both principles had been equally valid, then stacking would have worked.'

I defended myself and told them that the social proof suggestions – those delivered by the other participants – also had a compliance that was significantly higher than zero. Therefore, the social proof argument did change the opinions of participants. Additionally, I argued that participants in group 3 could have just ignored the 'bad' principle but clearly they did not: their compliance decreased.

But, my responses were to no avail. The audience remained unconvinced. They wanted to see an experiment in which both the social proof argument and the authority argument were equally effective. They were not convinced by the data, perhaps because the message they displayed is counter-intuitive to many. I now had two experimental studies, the one by Barry and Shapiro and my own study, but I was unable to convince the audience that the current practice of stacking was ineffective.

After we got home Steven and I decided to make our findings more convincing. We changed the implementation of our principles. We tried to make the social proof argument stronger by changing its wording. And we tried to make the authority argument less influential. We tried many small changes to the wording of the messages and eventually succeeded in making both strategies equally effective: the participants in group 1 would now receive a suggestion from previous participants who had been described as very successful at making the list, and the participants in group 2 would receive advice, not from a survival expert, but from a medical doctor. The successful previous participants proved more persuasive than the general previous participants, and the doctor proved less persuasive than the survival expert. This led to compliance scores in group 1 and group 2 that were very similar.

We replicated the experiment, but now with our new messages. We knew group 1 and group 2 would score similarly because we had extensively tested the messages. However, the interest was in group 3: did stacking two equally successful principles improve compliance?

What we found was surprising: the compliance in group 3 hardly differed from the compliance in the other two groups. Thus, even when two strategies were equally successful, their effects certainly did not 'stack up': we do not become more persuasive by stacking. Actually, the two experiments jointly give a consistent result: Stacking is as effective as the least effective message. If both of the messages are equally persuasive, then stacking will not help at all; it will just get you to the same result that you would have obtained when choosing only one principle.

STACKING PERSUASION PRINCIPLES ONLINE
Despite the fact that Steven and I strengthened our own confidence, we did not forget the disappointing experience at the conference. And most probably our last study would still not convince all our critics. Likely our critics would want to see more. They would like, as is quite standard when studying a new phenomenon, proof of the same finding in a different context. So, we decided to add one more experiment. This time we would test the same question, multiple or single principles, in a different context.

For our new study we wanted to show the effect of stacking principles not just in the laboratory, where respondents had to imagine a survival situation, but rather in real life. We wanted to show the effects of single or multiple persuasion strategies in the big bad world.

We decided on the following set-up: Steven and I would place a lot of Google Ads to recruit people to participate in a scientific study. The ad would say: 'Would you like to participate in a scientific study?' After clicking the ad, participants were linked to a website on which they had to rate a series of pictures. For each picture participants had to indicate the emotion that it invoked when they looked at it.*

In reality we were not at all interested in the emotional assessment of the pictures. Rather, we were interested in the effect of the

---

* This is a method that was suggested to me by Robbert Winkel and Thijs Waardenburg.

Google Ad. We were able to determine for each ad the number of people that saw it (views), and the number of people that clicked on it (click). This allowed us to measure the overall effect of the ad: for each Google Ad that we placed we were able to estimate the number of clicks per 1,000 views. The more clicks per 1,000 views, the more persuasive the ad would be.

We tried a large set of different ads. The main message – participate in a scientific study – never changed. What changed were the persuasion principles. We included scarcity – 'This experiment is only available for the next 18 hours'. We also included multiple authority ads like 'Professor Ford encourages you to participate in this study'. And, finally, we included social proof ads: 'Hundreds of others have participated in this study'. In addition to these simple single principle persuasive attempts we also placed ads that would combine two or three principles. Thus, the ad would, for example, say: 'This study is only available for the next 18 hours, hundreds of others participated, and Professor Ford recommends it'. We tried many different versions and we tried to control the length of the messages as much as possible. We also controlled the location in which we placed the ad on the Internet and on specific websites. We tried to make sure, as far as possible, to estimate only the effect of stacking principles for online persuasion.

The results were very clear. In all cases the ads with a single principle were more successful than the combinations of several principles. The most successful ad that used a combination of principles was about as successful as the least successful ad that contained only one strategy. This time the results were not artificial, and they were obtained by testing hundreds of thousands of people in a real situation rather than by testing dozens of people in a laboratory. The click-through rate, the number of people who clicked the ad divided by the number of people who viewed the ad, differed greatly between ads. On average,* the click-through rate of the multiple principle ads was 18%.** The click-through rates for

---

* Thus averaged over all multiple principle ads that we tried in the experiment.

** Yes, that's pretty low. However, it's quite common for online ads.

the average single principle ads was 36%. That's twice as effective by not stacking the principles!

Because we tested so many ads, we could derive a very general conclusion. The effects we were seeing were not specific to one ad, but rather they were true for multiple versions of single or multiple principle ads. Time after time, the use of a single principle was more effective than the use of multiple principles. Our two survival studies, the results by Barry and Shapiro and our ad study, all pointed in the same direction. Now we had a convincing story: Cialdini's persuasion principles definitely work, but we cannot just stack all of them. To create real impact we should carefully pick and choose the principles that we use.

BACK TO THE CONFERENCE

When we attended the conference the following year, our conclusions were met without skepticism. With our new evidence, we were able to convince the critics that indeed multiple principles stacked were less effective than a single well-chosen persuasion attempt. However, we knew in advance that it would not be sufficient to just demonstrate this empirically:* beside the results from our studies, we needed to have a theoretical mechanism by which the results could be explained. For many it did not feel right that principles could not be stacked. So, such a counter-intuitive finding demands an explanation. As scientists should, Steven and I started thinking about possible explanations for our effect.

Based on the extensive literature on the effects on persuasive communication, we tried to come up with plausible mechanisms by which the stacking of influence principles could reduce their effectiveness. We actually came up with two plausible mechanisms, and currently we still need to determine which one is true. However, you will probably be able to follow both ideas, and I hope that putting them forward makes the counter-intuitive conclusion that less persuasion leads to more compliance, a bit more intuitive.

For the first explanation we should return to the ideas we discussed in Chapter 5. There we discussed that there are two ways in

---

* By 'empirical' I am referring to 'solely based on data'.

which people process information. We saw that information can be processed using evolutionary click-zoom reactions, which we called System I or peripheral processing. But it can also be processed using a more rational approach, which we called System II or central processing. However, in Chapter 5 we also saw that a message will not merely have an effect by means of one of the processing routes, but the message itself can influence the processing route. When we discussed the ELM, I showed that specific messages, time constraints, or personalities influence which processing system is most likely used. The idea that messages can influence the processing system that is used is the core of one of the two explanations.

In the bookstore I saw *The Emperor's New Mind* being recommended as the 'Staff's' choice. This is what initially caught my intention, and almost persuaded me to buy the book directly. The effect of the authority principle in this initial case was primarily via System I: I did not wonder about the taste of the Staff, but rather I took the argument for granted. Click. Zoom.

However, by the time I got to the second display table for the 'Special Discount' books, things had changed. While the argument appealed to me, the argument also got me thinking. Quite literally: The argument had pushed me to make greater use of system II. I now started evaluating the principles and, instead of a click-zoom response, I started contemplating the pros and cons of the product. So, while the authority argument had exactly the persuasive effect it was intended to have, the second argument had a very different effect. The second argument pushed me to use more deliberate cognitive processing. Because of this, the effect of the persuasion principles was changed.

The idea that stacking principles alters the information processing was easy to accept for theorists since it was in line with earlier theories that relied on the ELM. However, I myself was not completely happy with this explanation. I think we always use both systems, but only alter how much each system is used. Hence, I think persuasive arguments are always at least partly processed by System I. And, even more, if the persuasion principle is genuinely a good argument, then it should have an effect via System 2 as well. And hence stacking should work in some situations at least. Despite this explanation sounding plausible, it is definitely not fault-proof.

Steven and I conjectured a second explanation that I myself find more plausible. I should again remind you that we don't yet have the data to prove it. The argument however is intuitive. It builds on one of the strongest ideas in social psychology called the 'negativity bias'.* The negativity bias implies that people tend to weigh losses more heavily than gains. So, a positive experience is enjoyed for a short time, but a similar negative experience has a much bigger impact. We have already seen an example of this in the previous chapters: People are unhappier when they lose 10 USD than happy when they win 10 USD. The negativity bias merely extends this idea to all kinds of experiences: in general negative experiences will weigh more heavily than positive ones. Your impression of a new colleague, for example, will be much more influenced by a single negative experience than by all the positive experiences encountered before. This bias has been demonstrated in many different domains and is one of the most robust findings in social psychology.

So, how do we use the negativity bias to explain our experimental results? The idea is quite simple: I started thinking that people might differ in their preference for distinct persuasion principles. Even though, on average, authority arguments are effective, I believed there are some people who dislike authority arguments and respond negatively to them. This is something that at the time I had not experimentally figured out yet – we will actually get to that in the next Chapter. However, if it is true that people have distinct leanings towards various persuasion principles then the negativity bias can easily be used to explain the detrimental effect of stacking.

Supposing that for 600 out of 1,000 people seeing one of the Google Ads, the social proof principle was effective while for 400 the principle was not effective. This means that (let's keep it sim-

---

* Much has been written about the negativity bias. See for example Amabile & Glazebrook, 1982 or Fiske, 1980.

ple) 600 people click on the social proof ad. Now let's further suppose that a similar thing is happening for scarcity: 650 out of the
1,000 people who saw the scarcity ad were inclined to respond positively to that principle and click on the ad. This means that for the
scarcity ad, 350 people were not inclined to click. Now let's make
our final assumption: the 350 people who 'dislike' scarcity are not
the same people as the 400 who 'dislike' social proof.

If I had shown an ad with both strategies to this group of 1,000
people my results would have been different. Instead of a click
through of 60% from social proof or 65% from scarcity, I would
now have a group of 400 + 350 = 750 people who disliked at least
one of the arguments in the ad.* If we now apply the negativity bias
and assume that while the ad contains an argument that works
for these people, but that the argument that does not work weighs
more heavily, then we get to the result that in the case of stacking
only 1,000 − 750 = 250 people click on the add. Thus, combining
two generally successful ads could greatly lower the click-through
rate.

Obviously the above example is contrived. The sets of people
who dislike the scarcity principle and who dislike the social proof
principle are likely to overlap. Furthermore, the negativity bias is
likely not so strong that any argument that people dislike will fully
determine whether they comply. However, the example does explain how individual differences in preferences for distinct strategies, in combination with the negativity bias, might explain the
negative results of stacking.

I was. at that moment, very pleased with this second explanation. However, the first one aligned much more with existing theories: the work on the ELM was very well developed, while there
was hardly any work examining individual differences. So, Steven
and I ended up publishing the first explanation.** But, the thought
of further examining the individual differences kept nagging me!

---

* Obviously this is an over-simplification: in reality the two groups likely
overlap. However, it illustrates the principle.
** See: Kaptein, Duplinsky & Markopoulos, 2011. The ad study can be
found in Kaptein & Duplinsky, 2012.

THE DIFFERENCE BETWEEN AN IMPLEMENTATION AND A
PRINCIPLE

Before we examine individual differences in responses to strategies in the next chapter, I want to discuss one more surprising finding that we observed from the first experiments described in this chapter. I did not focus on this result when discussing the studies, since I wanted to focus on the effects of stacking. However, the finding is too important to leave out, especially if you ever intend to use persuasion yourself in communication.

During the two survival experiments we used different implementations of the same principle. For example, look at the two versions of the social proof argument that we used:

> *You will see tips based on the responses of previous participants in this study.*

or

> *You will see tips based on the <u>successful</u> responses of previous participants in this study.*

When I compared the data of these two studies exact but for this change, I noticed that the effect of the first version was about half of that of the second version: thus, the second implementation was far more effective.* This being true, despite the fact that both of the above messages implemented social proof.

Although this finding does not affect our conclusions about stacking, it does explain why it is so hard to predict people's responses to persuasion: apparently the way you implement a persuasion principle can have a dramatic effect on the effectiveness of the message.

While this surprised me at first, in hindsight it is not really surprising. This exact difference is probably what sets apart good salesmen from the poor: while all know the tricks, only the good

---

* Note that both had a significant impact on the ratings. Their strength differed, but both implementations were successful.

salesmen are able to implement them well.

The large difference that emerges between implementations of a single strategy unfortunately complicates our understanding of the effects of psychological influence. If the differences in the effect of a principle can be so large, then how useful can it be to group them into principles? The grouping might be useful for remembering and summarizing, but if the effects of messages change considerably, even within a principle, then perhaps we do not have a correct grouping of influence attempts. It would only be feasible if we could use our grouping to predict the effects of different messages. This seems not to be the case given the large differences an implementation can make. If our grouping fails however, then our quest for increasing impact of mediated communication might also fail: if successful persuasion can only be attained by the magic of the good salesman, then how can we ever teach computers to use persuasion?

This chapter has answered a number of questions about stacking influence principles, and I hope it has given you a better understanding of the reasons why psychological influence works. However, we also added a number of new questions:

- Are the differences between people so large that the negativity bias can explain the negative effects of stacking?
- Is our grouping into principles really useful? Can we use this grouping to predict the effects of influence attempts?

In the next chapter we will see that these questions can be answered simultaneously.

WHAT HAVE WE LEARNED?

Before continuing with an examination of individual differences in the effects of persuasion, let's take one step back. Practically, the findings presented in the previous two Chapters show that psychological influence can have a considerable effect on our behavior. Moreover, we discussed six distinct principles of psychological influence: these are easy to remember ways in which you, as an influencer, can become more successful. We saw that implementations of these principles increased the impact of face-to-face communication, and we even saw examples in which persuasion increased the effect of computer-mediated communication and online campaigns. Thus, you can directly apply the knowledge of persuasion principles to your influence attempts.

This chapter however added a vital ingredient. We showed that it is not always a good idea to use all the persuasion you can think of at once. This however is the current practice: most book covers in stores right now seem to put up as many persuasive arguments as possible. And we also find that many e-commerce websites use a multitude of persuasion principles. Those who try to persuade us online seem to think that the more persuasion they use the better. This however is not true. So, you will have to make a choice: you will have to test specific implementations and finally select the one that is most effective for you.

This last sentence presents the main conclusion of this Chapter. Professor Cialdini gave us a great way to structure and classify influence attempts, a structure that can be used to create new implementations. But the current knowledge in social science is far from able to guarantee success. We do not yet understand how different implementations increase and decrease impact. We are not yet able to predict the effects of distinct messages. Thus, we will always need to measure the effects of new messages and we need to be open to changing our approach. If you are applying persuasion principles in practice, you will need to keep testing and improving. Fortunately, this is exactly what interactive technologies enable us to do: we can directly measure the effects of different messages that we feed to customers and change these messages accordingly.

SUMMARIZING

In this chapter, I elaborated on the effects of the six weapons of influence as presented by Professor Cialdini. Specifically, we examined whether we should use as much persuasion as we could think of, or rather select distinct principles. This chapter provided the following answers:

- Persuasion principles indeed increase the likelihood that people will exhibit a certain behavior: they will increase the impact. However, the use of several principles at the same time will lead to an impact that is no greater than the impact of the least successful principle.
- The use of several principles is probably not effective because it leads to the use of System II, and consequently lowers the number of click-zoom reactions.
- The negativity bias may also explain why the use of multiple principles is not effective, given the assumption that there are large individual differences in the effects of persuasion.
- There are large differences in the effects of different implementations of a particular principle. The effectiveness of different implementations should therefore be tested before use.
- We need to find out whether there are indeed large individual differences and how these relate to the effects of different implementations.

8

ALL FOR ONE AND ONE FOR ALL?

Last week my girlfriend, Rosa, bought two different coloured pants:[*] *a red and a green pair. I cannot say that I find them very attractive, but they surely are in fashion: The day after my girlfriend bought the pants I walked into the supermarket to find quite a number of women in brightly colored pants. In a single trip I counted eight of them.*

Now, for you the reader, it is hard to judge whether eight is a lot. There might have been thousands of women in my supermarket that day, and so it would not be bad at all if only eight of them wore colored pants. However, this was not the case at all. I reckon I saw about thirty women during my trip to the supermarket, and thus over 25% were wearing colored pants.

My girlfriend had decided to buy the pants two days earlier at her friend's birthday party. Although the brightly colored pants had been on the street for a while, the fact that she saw four of her twelve friends at the party wearing brightly colored pants made them a must-have for her as well. Apparently my girlfriend is reasonably susceptible to social proof. She likes to look at what others are doing or explain her own behaviors by recognizing that others are doing the exact same thing.

I personally seem to be a bit less influenced by social proof, although certain implementations surely work: It can certainly be a strong in-

---

[*] Obviously it's a bit more than a week ago: it was a week before I wrote the Chapter, not before you are reading it. At the time colored pants were still somewhat hip.

fluencer. However, in the bookstore I generally avoid the bestseller table. I try to find products that are, at least in my own eyes, a bit more special. Also, I am generally quite critical of arguments stating the 'everyone else is doing this or that…' This last reasoning really annoys me, probably because my dad used to always ask me: 'If everyone else jumps in front of a train, would you follow?' Perhaps that upbringing has weakened the effects of social proof for me. *

Rosa and I differ quite a bit in our susceptibility to specific persuasion principles. In Chapter I, I put forward individual differences in responses to persuasive strategies as a possible explanation for the negative effects of stacking persuasive arguments. In this Chapter we will further explore individual differences in responses to persuasion. In all fairness, it is obvious that there are differences between people: look around you; we clearly aren't all exactly the same. However, what we will try to examine in this chapter is the magnitude of differences in the effects of persuasive strategies. And, we will try to see whether we can measure and better yet predict these differences.

EVERYONE IS DIFFERENT

When I first became interested in possible individual differences in responses to persuasion, I again tried searching scientific literature. Contrary to my previous effort when searching literature for the effects of stacking, however, this time there was quite a lot was known about individual differences in the effects of persuasion. Hence, I had quite a lot of material to build on.

Some of the most famous studies on individual differences in the effects of persuasion have been carried out by Petty and Cacioppo, the creators of the Elaboration Likelihood Model (ELM) that we discussed earlier.** In their studies regarding the effect of

---

* After reading this intro my girlfriend requested me to alert you – the reader – to the fact that she also likes buying clothes when she's traveling abroad: She likes to buy clothes that are not easily available back home. Hence, scarcity is also effective for her.

** More about the ELM can be found in: Cacioppo & Petty, 1982; Cacioppo, Petty & Kao, 1984; and Haugtvedt, Petty & Cacioppo, 1992.

persuasive messages, they soon found out there were considerable differences in the responses of their experimental participants. For example; while on average authority arguments seem to increase compliance, it was clear that not everyone obeyed authorities. Actually, this was not very surprising: even in the classical Milgram experiments on the effects of authority, there were quite a substantial number of participants who did not fully comply.

However, these individual differences make it quite difficult to predict the outcome of an attempt to influence. Even more worrying, these individual differences seemed to lead to different outcomes of studies into the effects of persuasion. This motivated Petty and Cacioppo to look for ways in which it was possible to predict the outcomes of an influence attempts on individuals. They looked for differences between people that might explain their responses.

Originating from their own theory (the ELM), Petty and Cacioppo came up with the idea that different people might have a different inclination to use either central or peripheral processing. Thus, some people genuinely like to ponder on problems and weigh all the pros and cons. These people are inclined to use central processing while others are not really thinkers; they do not like to solve puzzles or ponder, and they resort more easily to peripheral processing.

Petty and Cacioppo called this new tendency, or trait, the 'need for cognition': people who scored highly on the need for cognition resorted to central processing, while those low on the need for cognition resorted more often to peripheral processing. Petty and Cacioppo designed a questionnaire that would measure a person's need for cognition. By indicating whether or not you agree to eighteen statements such as: 'I prefer complex to simple problems' and 'Thinking is not my idea of fun', your need for cognition can be assessed. After filling out the eighteen questions it is possible to compute your need for cognition score.

The score subsequently assists in predicting responses to persuasion. People who score very highly on the need for cognition seem to be less influenced by the use of persuasive arguments. authority arguments, for example, only work for those people who score highly in the need for cognition if the authority is genuine. So if using central processing makes the authority argument a good one, then it works. However, if this is not the case, the effect of using an authority argument is negative. This is contrary to those who score low on the need for cognition. For these people, authority arguments always have a positive effect. These people seem to show more click-zoom reactions: through peripheral processing the authority argument always works.

The need for cognition shows that there are indeed differences between people in their responses to influence attempts. However, the need for cognition is not sufficient to explain why Rosa likes to hang around the Bestsellers, and I do not. It also does not really help us explain why we should not stack the persuasive principles. Since the need for cognition identifies our overall tendency to comply with any influence attempt using peripheral processing, it does nothing to make distinctions between persuasion principles at the individual level. Since there are differences between people in the processing of influence attempts, the need for cognition is insufficient to explain the effects of stacking. I had to look for individual differences at the level of distinct persuasive principles.

Continuing my search, I soon found another study by Professor Cialdini – indeed the same Professor who introduced the taxonomy of six persuasive principles. Prof. Cialdini had worked on a trait called 'preference for consistency'. This is defined as ones need or preference for consistency. Cialdini and colleagues conjectured that people differ in their preference for consistency, and that this could be measured using a questionnaire. They designed the questionnaire and in a subsequent study showed that your score on the preference for consistency scale can partially predict how you respond to influence attempts that use implementations of the commitment and consistency principle. The researchers showed that a widely used sales strategy coined the 'foot in the door' strategy (see also Chapter 6) is less successful amongst people who score low on the preference for consistency scale. If you do not really value consistency, then appealing to the commitments that you have made and the consistency of your own behavior is not very effective. The preference for consistency is not related to the need for cognition principle, and differences in responses to the commitment and consistency principle that could be explained using preference for consistency do not relate to differences in the other 5 principles. Thus, the preference for consistency is an example of differences between individuals in their responses to a specific persuasive principle. *

CAN YOU PREDICT YOURSELF?

The work by Petty and Cacioppo along with that of Cialdini and colleagues shows that people indeed differ in their responses to influence attempts. These differences, especially those at the level of distinct persuasive principles, might explain why stacking multiple persuasive principles is ineffective.

Regretfully however, the results of many of the studies into individual differences are not completely consistent. Quite often you will be able to find someone who scores high on the preference for consistency scale but does not comply with the foot-in-the-door technique. Some of the laboratory studies have been quite successful, in the sense that the trait was useful in predicting a subsequent response, but definitely not all of the studies showed the same consistent results. This makes the utility outside the laboratory of both the need for cognition as well as the need for consistency response questionable.

I discussed the conflicting findings in the literature with Dr. Dean Eckles during one of my trips to Stanford University. Unlike me, Dean was not at all surprised by the difficulty in predicting individual responses to persuasive attempts using measures of traits. Unlike the attempts by Cialdini and others, Dean believed that at least some people would be very bad at reporting their own tendencies to comply with distinct persuasion principles. The questionnaires, such as the preference for consistency scales, might not give a proper score to individuals since people

---

* For more info on 'preference for consistency', see: Cialdini, Trost, & Newsom, 1995. A number of other traits that influence the effects of persuasion are known. See for example: Baumeister & Leary, 1995; Jarvis & Petty, 1996; Nail et al., 2001; Viswanatian, 1997 and Webster & Kruglanski, 1994.

are largely unaware of their own click-zoom responses.

To illustrate the point, Dean explained the difference between so-called 'operative' measures of individual differences and 'meta-judgmental' measures: a difference I was unaware of despite my earlier studies of psychology. The distinction however is fairly simple: with meta-judgmental measures of individuals we ask people to judge themselves. For example, if you state how much you agree with the statement 'I prefer complex over simple problems' then you assess your own preferences and behaviors. You reflect back on the problems that you have tackled, and their difficulty. Then, you reflect on how much you liked the problems. Eventually you will summarize all of these thoughts into your response: you give a meta-judgment of your own need for cognition. This mental process is quite difficult and might not always lead to the correct answers.*

In contrast, operative measures are obtained in a different way. To obtain an operative measure of your need for cognition, I do not have to ask you to reflect on yourself but rather I observe what happens when this need is actually in play. For example, I could ask you to solve ten puzzles. You have a choice between various simple and hard puzzles. After you have worked on the ten puzzles, I can see whether you ended up choosing simpler or harder puzzles and I can use this fact to give you a need for cognition score. If you chose lots of hard puzzles, you get a high score, and for lots of simple puzzles you get a low score. This operative measure of your need for cognition is directly based upon your behavior as opposed to an assessment and summary of your past behaviors.

Dean told me that scores of individuals obtained using operative measures do not always correspond to scores obtained using meta-judgmental measures. The actual behavior of people does not always correspond to the scores they give themselves. In fact, it might happen that in a questionnaire people indicate that they do not really care about the opinions of others – and as such are not susceptible to social proof – but when the persuasive principle is actually used, they comply directly using a click-zoom re-

---

* The difference between meta-judgmental and operative measures is important when measuring traits. For a great discussion see: Bassili, 1996.

sponse. Dean thought that the difference between meta-judgmental measures and operative measures could possibly explain the poor predictive ability of the scores that were obtained using questionnaires. It could well be that these scores obtained in the questionnaire, being an evaluation and summary of one's own past behaviors, did not correspond to actual behavior. You might just not be very well able to reflect upon your own susceptibility to persuasion.

I was impressed by the explanation that Dean provided and he inspired me to look for operative measures of individual differences in responses to persuasion principles. If I could show, using operative measures, that there were indeed differences between people in their responses to specific persuasion principles, then I could explain the negative effects of stacking. And, perhaps even more importantly, we might even be able to use the scores obtained using operative measures to predict the effectiveness of future influence attempts.

WHEN DIFFERENCES ARE IMPORTANT

Up to this point I have discussed differences between people, and we have discussed the technical distinction between operative and meta-judgmental measures of these differences. However, before we continue to explore individual differences in responses to persuasion using operative measures, I wanted to take one step back. When we talk about differences between people we have to make a distinction between differences that are actually important and meaningful, and those that are not. This distinction is important since we would logically expect at least some degree of difference between individuals whatever our topic of study is. However in science we are generally not interested in showing a difference, but rather showing a meaningful difference. Only if the latter is present does it make sense to measure and explain the difference.

The easiest way of describing my own thinking about important versus unimportant differences is by means of an example. Let's take responses to influence attempts with the social proof principle as our topic of study: we want to know whether there are important differences between people in their responses to social proof. Prof. Cialdini showed that the message 'the majority of guests in this hotel reused their towels' was on average more successful than a simple message 'Please reuse your towel'. By on average I mean that when Prof. Cialdini compared two groups of people one group scored higher than the other. This obviously does not mean that everyone in the group for which social proof was used was more inclined to reuse his towel. This is exactly the point at which the difference between important and unimportant differences between individuals becomes clear.

Suppose that there is some probability that given the message 'Please reuse your towel' you actually comply. This probability likely depends on the number of days you have been staying at the hotel, whether or not you happened to drop your towel on the floor of the bathroom and a number of other things. However, we'll ignore all of those for now. Suppose your probability of towel reuse is .25 (or 25%). We would expect that on one out of four days you reuse your towel when you see the simple message. For convenience, we'll also assume, without loss of generality, that this is true for everyone. So, when the sign is shown without persuasion, the probability of reuse of a towel is .25 for everyone. Thus, on average towel reuse in this group will be 25 percent.

Now, consider what might happen when we use social proof to make the message more effective. We know from the previous studies that the average compliance – the average probability of towel reuse – goes up. Let's assume the probability goes up to about .3 (so the new compliance is 30 percent). For you specifically, it might be a little higher, say 31 percent, while for your neighbor the increase is to 29 percent. On average however we get to 30 percent. In this case there are individual differences which account for you scoring slightly higher than your neighbor. However, the individual differences are not very important: the effect of using social proof is positive for everyone, and the order of magnitude is also the same for everyone. Thus, despite differences between you and your neighbor, qualitatively the effect of social proof is the same. The differences are unimportant.

However, there could be situations in which the differences are important. This is a bit more complicated to explain since I would need a few more guests than just you and your neighbor. Suppose again the effect of social proof leads to increased compliance for you. Again, your probability is increased to 31. In contrast, next door the probability actually drops to only 19 percent and in the room next to that there is an increase to 45 percent. In the end, the effect on your neighbor for the social proof message is zero: he remains at 25 percent.

Now in this case the average effect of the social proof message is still the same: there is an increase from 25 percent to 30 percent. And once again, there are differences between individuals. However, this time the differences are important: for some people social proof has a positive effect, while for others the effect is negative. This is qualitatively a big difference. While on average social proof is effective, there are apparently people who are less likely to reuse their towels when this type of message is used than when it isn't. This individual difference clearly has implications: since social proof is ineffective for some, we should refrain from its use for them if we want to maximize towel reuse. This is an important difference between individuals in the effects of Social Proof.

LET'S FIND OUT

After discussing meta-judgmental and operative measures and possible individual differences in responses to persuasion, Dean and I were both interested in further examining the differences between people. We were both curious whether the differences would be important – as described above – or unimportant. However, we were unable to find previous research in which operative measures were used to examine individual differences. So we set out to study this ourselves. As both Dean and I were interested in the effects of influence and persuasion online, we decided to design a study that would allow us to investigate individual differences in responses to different persuasive principles in an online store.

Designing a good study proved quite challenging. We were thinking about using an online store to see how people would respond to sales attempts using different persuasion principles. We were interested in the effects of these principles on individuals: we

wanted to show that using authority on me increased my probability of a sale, while using the same principle on you decreased
it. Initially we thought we would offer you a book and see if you
wanted to buy it. We would then offer you a book stating that it
was 'Recommended by the Editors of *The New York Times*'. Obviously, this is not enough: the actual book that we use necessarily
affects your willingness to buy. It might even be the case that the
book itself plays a larger role in the purchase decision than the
persuasion principle that was used. So we had to come up with a
study design that allowed us to measure the effect of persuasion on
individuals, regardless of the products that were used.

We started by narrowing down the range of books that we
used: we created an online store that would only sell science fiction
books. We searched for books that were unknown, with the same
price tag and were equally appreciated by readers. In doing this we
tried to minimize the effects of the type of product. We filled our
store with a very homogenous selection of products.

Next we created multiple implementations for each persuasion
principle. We wanted to see multiple responses of everyone in our
study for each principle. By offering the same strategy many times,
using many implementations, we could better estimate the effect
of the principle as opposed to the specific implementation. We
created the online store in which each product could randomly be
coupled with each persuasive principle. Thus, the persuasion and
the product could be shown independently.*

Once we had filled our online store with homogenous books
and a number of implementations of persuasion principles, we invited people to take a virtual tour of the store and evaluate the
online store. During the tour however, we would ask people to rate
specific products: 'Would you buy this book?' and 'Would you
recommend this book to your friends?' The people evaluating the
store did not know the purpose of the study, and thus they were
not directly influenced by our choice of persuasive principles: the

---

* For those interested: to further control for the effect of the product we
randomized the persuasive principles over the products, and randomized the
order of the products.

store and its evaluation mimicked as well as possible the effect persuasion principles would have in a true online store.

After a while we ended up with more than 150 people who had each evaluated at least twelve books: nine books with persuasion principles, and three books without.* The books that were pitched using persuasion principles used different implementations of the social proof principle, the authority principle, or the scarcity principle. This gave us a dataset that allowed us to finally examine the individual differences in the effects of persuasion principles. Let's run through the results of the study.

First of all, we found that books that were offered using a persuasive principle on average scored higher than those pitched without the use of persuasion. On average the books supported by any of the 3 persuasion arguments scored higher than the books without any arguments. This result is not very surprising: we just replicated the findings by Cialdini and many others that persuasion is effective. So yes, using persuasive principles on average increased people's willingness to buy books. This is why persuasion principles are also known as 'weapons of influence': they increase impact. It was however reassuring to see that our online store really worked.

The second result was much more surprising. Now that we had seen multiple responses to each persuasion principle per person we were able to determine the effect of the persuasion principle for distinct individuals. This allowed us to directly examine whether the differences between people in their responses to persuasion were important or not. And, much to our own surprise, the differences were huge and clearly important. For example, The differences that we found for social proof – the principle with the largest average effect in our store – was negative for over 30% of the people in our study. Thus, although social proof was on average very effective, almost one third of the people in the study were more likely to buy a book when we did not show the social proof argument than

---

* We ended up using only a selection of the six persuasive principles since some principles, such as liking, are less straightforward to implement online.

when we did. That is a tremendous difference! All of these people were apparently less willing to buy bestsellers than other types of books that were not. This was my first concrete proof that my own response in the physical bookstore is not uncommon: many others like me do not like bestsellers.

We obviously did not use three principles just for fun. The fact that people differ tremendously in their responses to social proof does not necessarily mean that there are differences at the level of different persuasive principles. It might be the case that the people who respond negatively to the Social Proof principle also respond negatively to authority and scarcity principles. Then, our finding would only imply that people differed in their general tendency to comply with persuasion. That would not be sufficient to explain the negative effect of stacking principles (see Chapter 7).

Dean and I decided to zoom in further. We calculated the effect of each persuasion principle for each person in our online store. This allowed us to not only see that the responses to persuasion were often negative, but also allowed us to see the relationships between the different principles. We could, for example, direct-ly examine whether or not people who did not respond to social proof did respond to scarcity. This gave us our second surprising result: most people for whom social proof was ineffective, one of the other persuasion principles was effective. So, we were not look-ing at a general tendency to comply with persuasion, but rather at important individual differences in responses to distinct persua-sive principles! Finally I had all the results I needed to explain the negative effects of stacking persuasive principles.

THINK AGAIN

Just as Steven and I had done when we first found our stacking results, Dean and I decided to present our results to a group of re-searchers. This time the results were presented not at a conference but rather at the lab meeting of Professor Clifford Nass at Stanford University, where both Dean and I worked at the time. We were very excited about sharing our findings.

One of the people in the audience was a super bright Ph.D student of Clifford's called Abhay Sukumaran. Abhay has done quite a lot of research into influence and persuasion himself and he knows all the theories that are intended to explain the effects of persuasion principles. When we were pitching our results to Abhay, he himself was researching different environmental or contextual factors that influenced the success of various influence attempts.

While Abhay was initially impressed by our findings and the design of our online store, he did not agree with our final conclusions. Dean and I were shocked. Where were we wrong in our thinking? Why did our results not show stable differences between individuals in their responses to persuasion? We both knew that Abhay was extremely good at finding alternative explanations for the observations of scientific studies and this was very worrying: had we overlooked one of the possibilities?

'Some emotions or moods can play a role in the influence process...' Abhay said to start his alternative explanation. He continued with a rather difficult theoretical explanation that I will spare you. But I will try to summarize the main idea: previous research had shown that some persuasion principles are either more or less effective when people are in a certain mood.[*] For example, people who are happy are more affected by persuasive attempts than people who are sad. Apparently happy people have a tendency to use more peripheral processing (System 1) than those who are sad. And, there are even more detailed studies that show the effect of moods on distinct principles, not just on the overall effect of influence principles. According to Abhay this was the explanation for our results. During our study some people – for one reason or another – were happy while others were sad. The moods of the people browsing our study differed. This temporary difference in mood is what caused the differences in the effects of persuasion principles. We had not controlled for this. So what we believed to be stable individual traits – true stable differences in responses to persuasion – could actually just be caused by very fleeting and temporary differences in mood. We found the differences because

---

[*] To read about emotion and persuasion see: Bless, Bohner, Schwarz & Strack, 1990.

ours was a snapshot in time, not because of genuine differences between people.[*]

Dean and I had very few arguments to refute Abhay's alternative explanation. While we knew that much of the research on differences in the effects of persuasion relied on questionnaires – such as the need for cognition – which had been shown to be pretty stable, this was only true for meta-judgmental measures. We had no idea whether or not differences obtained using operative measures would actually be stable over time. What we were interested in were stable differences not fleeting differences caused by a temporary mood.

As with the studies that Steven and I had carried out, Dean and I had to go back to the drawing board. How could we possibly prove that the differences we were looking at were stable rather than temporary?

During a BBQ in Palo Alto, a village close to Stanford University where Dean and I both lived at the time, Dean came up with an ingenious solution to our problem. This time we would replicate our study in the online store asking people to rate books at multiple points in time. We would ask people to come back to the online store once a week and rate a number of products. During each visit people would be confronted with multiple persuasive principles. This set-up would allow us to not only examine individual differences, but would actually allow us to see whether these differences were stable over several weeks.

This new study set-up however was obviously a bit tricky. We had to find people who were willing to come back to the website multiple times. Additionally, we had to expand our range of books and we had to expand the number of implementations of our persuasive principles. Dean and I stuck to the plan and designed a completely new, well-stocked, online bookstore. This time we made sure that the books and the persuasion principles

---

[*] People might hold the same emotions for a longer period of time. If this is true then it's hard to disentangle whether the individual differences are a state or a trait. Dean and I however were not necessarily interested in the theory behind traits and states; we just wanted to make sure that what we believed to be important differences actually was correct.

differed every time people came back to the store.

After weeks of measuring people's willingness to pay for specific products we finally had data that we could use to convince Abhay. Sure, he was partially right: some of the differences that we had found in the previous study did not last over time. Sometimes a principle worked better in the first week than in the second week. These differences were to be expected given studies with individual people: we rarely act precisely the same at two different points in time.

More importantly, however, we were able to see that besides the unstable, temporary differences, quite a lot of the individual differences lasted over time. For example, for many of the people visiting the store the order of the most effective principle did not change over time: if the authority principle was most effective in the first week this was also true in the second and the third weeks. We thus found stable individual differences in responses to distinct persuasive principles. This result is exactly what I needed to explain the negative effects of stacking using the negativity bias.

Our results showed that we could indeed use operative measures, direct responses to persuasion principles of people visiting an online store, to estimate individual differences. These estimates we could subsequently use to predict which persuasion principle would be most effective for individuals in the future. People did not have to fill in questionnaires for us to determine which types of persuasion would be effective. Purely based on your responses we can see which persuasion principles you are susceptible to.

GENERALLY APPLICABLE?
Now that Dean and I were quite sure that the differences we found were actually stable, there was still another point that Abhay had raised of which we were not yet sure. We were able, based on our study, to estimate the effect of distinct persuasion principles for individuals when we were trying to sell them books. However, we were unsure what the value of our estimates would be for different influence attempts. If you are likely to buy bestselling books – and thus you are susceptible to social proof – will you also be more likely to buy bestselling music albums? And, would you be more

willing to take your medication at the right time if this was supported by a social proof argument? Abhay was questioning whether the stable individual differences that we found would actually
generalize to other influence attempts.

Again, at another BBQ – the weather in Palo Alto is often quite
nice – we tried to find a way in which we could examine whether our results would generalize and whether or not the effects of
persuasion principles would be stable across different situations.
The solution to this was obvious: we had to repeat our study, but
this time not only for multiple time points but rather for multiple
situations.

To do so Dean and I created both a bookstore and an online
music store. The two stores were designed radically different, but
both used multiple implementations of persuasive principles.
Once done, I invited people to judge our bookstore and the books
that we were selling there. Then, Dean invited people to judge the
music albums that were sold in the music store. Due to the differences in design and the different origin of the invitation, people
participating in our study did not know that the data on the two
stores would be linked. Thus, if our results were shown to hold
over both stores, then the results could indeed be generalized and
they would not be the result of people's tendency to be consistent.
Our new set-up allowed us to examine whether or not the individual differences in responses to persuasive principles would generalize over different contexts.

Our results showed a clear relationship between the effect of
the principles that were used and the context that we were studying. Some principles proved more effective for selling books,
while other proved more effective for selling music albums. This
is not very surprising. However, we also found a lot of stability
of the effects of principles at the individual level. If you are more
sensitive than others to scarcity arguments in the bookstore, then
you are also likely to be more sensitive than others to scarcity
when buying music albums. Thus, if we know how you respond
in one specific store, we can use this information to predict how
you will respond to the same persuasion principle in a new online
store. The context does affect the average success of distinct prin-

ciples, but the way you responded compared to other people was stable over contexts.

IMPLEMENTATIONS OF PERSUASION PRINCIPLES

In the previous Chapter we raised not only the question of individual differences, but also questions about the usefulness of the taxonomy of six persuasion principles as provided by Cialdini. We saw that the average effect of different implementations of the same principle could differ tremendously. This makes you wonder whether or not the grouping into principles is actually useful for predicting responses. It might be that if the individual differences are at the level of implementations rather than principles, that the use of general principles of persuasion is limited.

To understand this in more detail, please consider the following two implementations of the scarcity principle which you might encounter when browsing a website:

> *Implementation 1: This T-shirt is almost sold out. Order it right now!*

or

> *Implementation 2: We only have a few T-shirts left in stock. Order yours before it's too late!*

The question is whether or not someone who responds positively to the first implementation also responds positively to the second. If this is the case, then it is useful to call both of them implementations of the scarcity principle. However, if this is not the case, and the response to the first implementation is totally not predictive of the response to the second, then the grouping into scarcity is not very useful.

The data that Dean and I collected could in part be used to answer this question. We were able to compare the effects of a specific implementation of – for example – the scarcity principle with the effects of different implementations of that principle. We could do this not only for scarcity, but also for the other strategies.

This showed that people responded quite consistently within the different principles. Thus, using the principles as a grouping level was useful in predicting future responses. The taxonomy of six persuasion principles, while perhaps not the only possible useful taxonomy of persuasive implementation, was at least useful. *

PREDICTING INFLUENCE

In this Chapter I have discussed the effects of persuasion principles on individuals. The studies show that there are important differences between individuals in their responses to persuasion. This has a very important result: if you want to predict the response of a person to an attempt of influencing it is useful to know his or her previous responses to the same persuasion principle.

Whereas this result may be somewhat trivial, it is very important. We are still trying to understand the effects of persuasion principles and how these might improve the impact of online communication. However, all the psychological explanations that we have discussed were based on groups of people: they all concerned average effects. A positive average effect of persuasion is likely a guarantee that if you use persuasion principles on large groups of customers you will make more money than if you do not. However, it is not at all a guarantee that a specific influence attempt using that persuasion principle will have a positive effect on a specific individual customer. Indeed, Dean and I had shown that some persuasive attempts, while effective on average, might be detrimental for specific customers. Some people are just not inclined to buy bestsellers for instance.

When I first saw all these results together, I began to understand why our online impact is so low. We are applying persuasion techniques wrongly online. While we are using the same influence strategies that good salesmen do, we use them in a very naïve fashion. We stack all of our attempts, even though this is largely ineffective. And, we use the same persuasion principle for everyone, even though this is definitely not the most effective approach for each individual customer. Real sellers – those excelling offline

---

* For a full description of this work please see: Kaptein & Eckles, 2012.

– use persuasion sparingly. And they will adapt their principles to their audience. This is what we will need to do in online communication if we want to have impact online.

SUMMARIZING

In this chapter I have looked at differences between people and the effects of the use of persuasion principles on them. Although individual differences are a logical explanation for the negative effect of stacking influence principles (Chapter 7), there was little direct evidence for the existence of such differences. Previous researchers had already shown that certain personality traits – such as the need for cognition – led to differences in influence. Now Dean Eckles and I have added the following to it:

- There are big – important – differences in the way people react to persuasion principles.
- Although persuasion principles are often effective on average, they will have a negative effect on a proportion of your customers. (Some people just do not do what others do…)
- People are consistent in their response to persuasion principles, both over time and over different contexts as well.
- A person's previous response to a persuasion principle is a pretty good predictor of his future response.
- To really have an impact at the individual level, you will need to select the correct persuasion principle.

In the next chapter I will show how you, just like a good seller, can select persuasion principles for individuals. With the right technologies, we can use persuasion online as effectively as we do offline.

9

PERSUASION PROFILES

Most of the salespeople at my favorite bookstore know what types of books I like by now. I like popular science books, statistics books, and perhaps a Philosophy book here and there. But some of the smarter salespeople also know which persuasion principles I am susceptible to: they know the arguments they can use to influence me to buy a book. For example, they know that I rarely take home bestsellers, but I can appreciate a special offer.

This primarily means that I walk into the bookstore all too often. However, it also shows that some sellers keep a mental picture of their customers. At least, of those customers who frequent their stores. They keep a sort of profile of my tastes, and a summary of the arguments that they can use to persuade me.

The profile kept by a seller might largely be unconscious but it is still a profile: it is a collection of knowledge about me specifically. The seller can use this profile to tailor his pitch to my needs, find the right products, and eventually use the right persuasion principle to close the deal.

The mental profile that the seller keeps is distinct from the profiles that we traditionally think about in classical marketing: The seller likely does not think that there are two (or three or four) distinct types of customers. Rather, they are likely to have a unique image of each of the regular customers. In this chapter we will examine how technology can keep a similar mental profile of each individual customer to eventually increase the effect of online communication.

In the previous chapters we learned the following:

1. Persuasion principles are very effective and may offer the solution to the problem of the low impact of online attempts to influence.
2. We cannot use all the persuasion principles simultaneously. Stacking does not work.
3. There are large and consistent individual differences in reactions to persuasion principles.

To really have an impact, we need to know more. What we need is to understand how we are able to apply the above conclusions to technologies. We have a number of theoretical findings, and we know the structure of psychological influence – the six principles. However, this is only the first step. We now know that we must find proper implementation of the right principle for every individual customer who we want to influence. This is exactly what good offline salespeople do. The problem is that it takes a few more steps to really implement this in interactive technologies. In this chapter I will discuss how interactive technologies can use persuasion profiles to become as effective as their human counterparts.

PERSONALIZATION

Personalization, the adaptation of messages to individuals – even in interactive technologies – has been common practice for quite some time. Recommender systems (as discussed in Chapter 4) provide an example of personalization: recommender systems personalize the type of product or the product category that is shown to an individual customer. This type of personalization has already gone some way to improve the impact of online communication. In this section, however, we will take it a step further. We will focus on personalization and the means by which the attempt is made, rather than the end goal of the attempts to influence; the product offered.

Until recently many personalization efforts in marketing have been based on demographics – gender, age, post code – or information about your personality. Are you an introvert? Are you an extravert? The personalization process in marketing typically proceeds as follows:

1. The marketer, seller, or strategist divides customers into categories or groups. Depending on the type of division he chooses, there are more or fewer categories. For example, the marketer postulates that there are four types of customers: the young introvert, the old introvert, the young extravert, and the old extravert. * These types of customers can be identified by their background characteristics and their responses on a questionnaire. Recently, classification based on behavioral responses as opposed to questionnaire responses has been becoming a bit more common, but it is not yet commonplace.

2. The marketer envisions – sometimes with the help of some social scientific theory – what messages or ways of offering a product suit which type of customer: the young introvert prefers to see lots of pictures, while older extraverts like to see textual descriptions of products. **

3. New customers are classified into one of the selected customer types, as fast as possible, and for the rest of their lives are confronted with the communication style the marketer deemed correct for that customer type.

This approach to personalization has some logical flaws. First, it is unlikely that there are only a small number of 'types' into which all customer customers fit. The more customers you have, the more customer types you are likely to have. Assigning a specific person to a specific category often involves basic errors. Even worse, the link between the content – for example the lengthy textual description – and the customer type is often erroneous as well.

---

* Many marketers seem to like giving specific names to these types of customers. We might have red, yellow, and blue customers. Or we could find Linda, John, and Alex.
** An example of these kinds of differences in offering products can be found in: Hauser, Urban, Liberali & Braun, 2009. These authors however do not stick to a distinct number of customer types and dynamically adapt their content to individuals. This is a must read paper for online marketers.

Perhaps old extraverts like pictures too. And, likely, not all young introverts like pictures. Hence, the categorization into a limited number of types coupled with content for each customer type in practice often fails.

The idea of assigning individuals into groups of customer types originated from the inability of marketers – or anyone really – to remember hundreds of different types of customers. If you identify twenty different customer types, that is already a difficult number to recall. Additionally, the method of reducing the number of customer types was also driven by the limited amount of data marketers had available on specific customers. Historically marketers often had access to some simple demographics, and that information had to be used as efficiently as possible. Creating prototypes is a pretty good idea when humans have to remember them and limited information is available.

Times have changed. Marketers do not have to remember customer types themselves; computers can aid them. Computers have no trouble remembering millions of different customer types. The problem has shifted from identifying different customer types to identifying distinct pieces of content: if you only have pictures or text available, then often it's much easier to map people directly to the content than to map them to customer types and subsequently map these customer types to the content. Digital customers – yes, that's you – can be tracked and logged everywhere. Your product preferences are known; your responses to persuasion can be determined; your past purchases are known; and your location at any point in time is known. Your previous responses to content can be used directly to select the best future content – without any interference from gender or age or some hypothetical customer type.

That all sounds pretty good (I hope), but how does it work in practice? What we want to do is select the 'best' persuasion principle for an individual customer. By the this I mean the principle that is most effective. So, for afew years I have been working to find a successful way to directly map customer behavior to a choice of persuasion principles. Let me take you on my quest.

SUSCEPTIBILITY TO PERSUASION

I started out with relatively simple experiments to prove that personalization of persuasion principles was indeed effective. Actually, my first experiments in this direction much reflected old marketing habits: they used a priori measurements of traits that were subsequently coupled to content.

My first study in this direction was actually a side project that was coupled to a larger research project I was involved in at the time: investigating people's responses to chat robots – a project I will not detail here. * However, during one of these studies I also slipped in a number of questions addressing people's susceptibility to persuasion principles. For example I asked people to state whether or not they agreed with statements like 'I always listen to the advice of my general practitioner', and 'If a product is almost sold out, I want to buy it.'

The people participating in the study about the chat robot filled in these questions not knowing how they related to the study. The questions were buried in between a number of questions about their personality. However, the scores on the questions allowed me to calculate a rudimentary susceptibility to persuasion score for each participant for different principles. The first question mentioned above measured people's susceptibility to authority, while the second measured susceptibility to scarcity. I added multiple questions for each principle and combined the responses into a susceptibility score for each principle for each person. If you agreed with all the authority statements, your susceptibility to authority score would be high; likewise for the other strategies.

By the end of the study however we (research is seldom conducted alone) asked the unsuspecting participants to help us find more people to participate in the evaluation of the chat-robot. We asked people to provide us with the email addresses of others who might be likely to participate in the study too. Importantly, our request

---

* OK, then, just briefly: I was interested in whether simple (non-verbal) behavior of chat-robots could influence the perceptions of people regarding the robots. One of the studies found that if a robot takes as long to respond as the person took to type a question, then people think it is more intelligent than when it responds directly. Thus, it paid off to delay the answer: Kaptein, de Ruyter, Markopoulos & Aarts, 2009.

for email addresses was not the same for everyone: for some people we showed participants an authority argument to provide us with the addresses, while for others we used a scarcity argument. The results of this simple study were very clear: those people who scored high on susceptibility to authority provided more email addresses when we used the authority principle and vice versa. Thus, we could use the scores on the questionnaire to predict which persuasion principle would be most successful. This provided the first evidence that personalization of persuasion principles – this time based on a questionnaire – might be effective.

<h3 style="text-align:center">DISCOURAGING SNACKING</h3>

After this initial small success, Dr. Boris de Ruyter, one of the supervisors of my PhD research, and I decided to tackle a bigger challenge. Boris was involved in a study into people's snacking behavior: he was interested in reducing the number of snacks that people ate between meals. He wanted to find ways in which he could motivate people to lead a healthier life. He knew about my work on personalized persuasion and wondered whether it could be used to motivate people to snack less. We decided to work together on a study evaluating the use of personalized persuasion to encourage people to snack less.

The study Boris and I did was also modeled on the 'old' marketing method of personalization: we used a questionnaire to estimate the susceptibility of individuals and subsequently changed the messages we used based on the responses to the questionnaire. However, we started by extending and evaluating the short questionnaire used in the chat-robot study. We created a standardized measurement instrument to measure susceptibility to persuasion and subsequently evaluated it. By designing a standardized questionnaire we created the ability to structurally measure susceptibility to persuasive principles.

After developing the questionnaire, we administered it. We had hundreds of people fill out the susceptibility to persuasion scale (STPS). Next, we explained– using a website – what we meant by snacking behavior and then we asked them whether or not they would be willing to track the number of snacks they ate for two weeks. Every day they received a text message on their mobile phones to ask them about their snacking behavior. Every day participants were asked to reply with the number of snack they had eaten that day.

This is exactly what we did in the first week of the experiment. However, in the second week the set-up was more interesting: in the second week we sent two messages, one in the morning and one in the evening. The evening message would ask about the number of snacks, just as we did in the first week. The morning message, however, was intended to discourage snacking: in these messages we tried to motivate people to snack less.

Boris and I created many different text messages with different implementations of persuasion principles. This allowed us to match the message that we sent in the morning to the scores people had obtained on the susceptibility to persuasion scale they filled out before the experiment.

To test whether personalized persuasion was more effective than non-personalized persuasion we created a number of different groups within the experiment. One third of the participants received text messages that contained implementations of the persuasive principle to which they were most sensitive according to the questionnaire. One third however received exactly the opposite messages: these participants received implementations of those principles that they were least susceptible to. Finally, the last third of our participants received a random selection of a message each day: these participants could receive an implementation of any persuasion principle.

The results after a week of measurements were very clear: The text messages in the second week led to a decrease in the number of snacks people ate. This was true in all of the three groups in the experiment. However, the personalized messages were more effective than the random ones, which in turn were more effective than the 'contra'-personalized messages. The study thus showed that we were able to effectively motivate people to eat more healthily by applying personalized persuasion.[*]

---

[*] For a full description of this study see: Kaptein, de Ruyter, Markopoulos & Aarts, 2011.

Learning from past behavior

At a major scientific conference, Computer-Human Interaction (CHI), I spoke once again with Abhay Sukumaran. I told him about the results of the snacking study that Boris and I had done, and he seemed impressed. However, as before, he was skeptical. He said: 'It's great that you have been able to personalize persuasion based on questionnaires, but in practice that approach will likely fail. It will be hard to get people to fill out the questionnaires. What will you do if they don't? What messages would you then use?'

I knew he was right. Using the 'old' marketing approach was simple, but not likely to be very effective on a large scale. If we wanted to apply personalized persuasion on a large scale we could not depend on people's willingness to fill out questionnaires. Thus, I had to think of another approach: I had to look for a way in which persuasion could be personalized without the use of questionnaires. We ought to be able to select the right message based on observations that were readily available for everyone.

After the conversation with Abhay, I walked to the lobby of the Marriot Hotel in Atlanta – this was where the conference was being held. Upon approaching the lobby I noticed something: the lobby had two entry points, one served by a revolving door and the other one by a sliding door. I approached the sliding door, but just as I was about to enter I saw a little sign:

The management of this hotel kindly asks you to use the revolving door.*

Of course, I immediately recognized the authority principle in the message. And indeed, I took the revolving door.

The sign did get me thinking though. The Marriot hotel would find it hard to administer a questionnaire to all new visitors but

---

* In case you are wondering about the reason for such a message: it is pretty warm in Atlanta, so mostly the air-conditioning is turned on. The revolving door will let out less of the cold than the sliding door, and thus, to save energy, you are encouraged to use the revolving door.

it would not be at all hard to identify visitors and see whether or not they complied with the request on their sign. Additionally, the sign did not need to be a static piece of paper: it could also be a small monitor that could be used to display different messages. This simple set-up would offer the possibility for the hotel to try out different messages – each implementing different persuasion principles – and measure directly the response of individual visitors. By using this set-up the hotel could measure the effect of distinct persuasion principles without using a questionnaire. I began to wonder whether it would be possible to select the best persuasive principles purely based on these behavioral responses of visitors.

The problem is quite simple. Suppose you have three different messages, each implementing a different persuasive principle. You can show one of these messages every time a customer enters the hotel. Suppose these are the messages:

1. Would you please take the revolving door? 90 percent of our guests take the revolving door – Social proof
2. The management of this hotel kindly asks you to use the rotating door – Authority
3. Take the revolving door today. Now is your chance! – Scarcity

Once a visitor arrives at the door – and you recognize him, for example, based on face recognition or the Bluetooth key of his mobile phone[*] – you have to choose a message. I was wondering what the best policy would be for selecting the message. After showing the message it would be easy to measure the response – again by face recognition or Bluetooth – and use that information the next time the same visitor approached the doors. However, I was unsure how to best 'learn' the individual preferences based on the sequential observations.

---

[*] This is very possible. See for earlier applications: Kostakos, 2008.

THE IDEAS BEHIND SEQUENTIAL LEARNING

Now I pitched my newest problem to Abhay – how to learn from sequential observations of visitors approaching the sliding door. How could we choose a persuasive principle without having the luxury of questionnaires? Together, Abhay and I decided on a number of properties that the learning process should have.

First, we considered the number of successes of each message as a random variable* with an associated probability distribution. We considered the effect of the messages as variables whose outcome was uncertain but could be described by probabilities. Each message has a specific probability of being successful: the visitor using the revolving door. Thus our problem boiled down to learning these probabilities. If the social proof message has a probability of being successful score of .8 (or 80%), and the scarcity message a probability of .4 (40%) then we should obviously use the social proof message.

Estimating these probabilities is not at all hard. If we have one hundred people entering the hotel lobby who have been shown the social proof message, then estimating the probability is simple: we count the number of successful attempts to persuade the visitor to use the revolving door and divide this by the total number of visits. So, if eighty out of the hundred people end up taking the revolving door after seeing the Social Proof message then the probability of success for that message is 80/100=.8. This is just simple math.

However, if we only observe ten people, of which eight take the revolving door, than we arrive at the same figure: 8/10 = .8. While both situations result in an estimated probability of success for the social proof message of .8, these situations are distinct. In the case of one hundred observations, we can be quite sure of the fact that about 80% of the people take the revolving door after seeing the message. If we add one person and the attempt to influence is successful then we arrive at 81/101= .802: the estimated probability

---

* A random variable is a function that maps an event (for example tossing at least one heads when tossing two coins), out of all possible events, to a real number. The associated probability distribution is a function that maps these real numbers to numbers between 0 and 1 which, when added up over all possible events, comes to 1.

hardly changes. However, if that same person entered after we had observed only 10 people, than we would get a new estimate of 9/11= .82. The latter is quite a bit higher. Thus, if we have a small number of observations then the probabilities that we estimate for each message 'shift' more easily based on a single new visitor. The more people we see, the more confident we get and the less the estimate shifts. We also had to take this confidence into account.

We started from this basic principle: by counting successes we can estimate the success probability of each message. And, the more observations we obtain, the more confident we are in our estimate. We can then use these estimates to determine the next persuasion principle on the sign: if we are very confident that a social proof message is more effective than a scarcity message, we should choose the social proof message.

So far the discussion has focused on counting the successes for multiple visitors, In which case we are able to estimate the average effect of a message over a group of visitors. However, we have just learned that some persuasive principles work better for some people than for others. And to personalize our message we specifically want to identify these differences. There is an obvious way of doing this: Suppose that a new visitor arrives at the doors. Let us call her visitor 'V'. To determine which message is most effective for visitor V, it makes sense to look at the estimates of the effects of the message that we obtained for earlier visitors. This is all we know at that point in time. Let's assume, for example, that our estimate of social proof based on visitors prior to V was .8, that of Authority was .6, and that of Scarcity was .4. This information, gathered by looking at earlier visitors, provides a reasonable starting point for approaching visitor V. Based on the above estimates it sounds reasonable to present visitor V with the social proof message as this principle seems the most effective at that point. [*]

After showing the social proof message, we can observe the response of Visitor V. If, at this first visit, the social proof message is

---

[*] It seems evident that one should select the message that one believes to be most successful. However, this is not always the most feasible strategy. We will get back to this topic.

not effective, then that observation provides us with some knowledge about the average effect – over different people – of the social proof message. More importantly, it also gives us direct information about Visitor V. Our guess of the probability of success of the social proof message for visitor V should be lowered. By making sure that we start with a less confident estimate for visitor V than for the whole group, we can make sure that our estimate for visitor V changes more quickly than the estimate we maintain for the whole group. And, if we see visitor V again, we can again try out a principle and update our estimates. The more often we see visitor V, the more confident we get about her personal probabilities of success for the different messages. It is possible to maintain an estimate of the success of each specific persuasion principle for each individual person, and the confidence that we have in that estimate. As our estimates become more confident we can make better and better choices, for each individual, about the type of message we should use. In this way the system can learn, based on recurring interactions, which persuasion principle is most likely to be effective for an individual visitor. *

THE PERSUASION PROFILE

After Abhay and I discussed the ways in which we might be able to learn which message would work based on repeated observation, I flew back to Stanford. ** There, I told Dean about the idea of keeping track of the success of different messages for individuals and using those estimates to inform the selection of persuasive principles. By continuously updating our estimates we could become better and better at selecting the right message. He looked at me and started laughing. Initially I hoped the sudden joy was caused by my enthusiasm about the new idea, but I quickly learned that this was not the case. Dean told me that two years before I had started working with him, he himself collaborated with a Stanford

---

* There are a few more tricks one can use to derive a better estimate for individuals by using the estimates of the average effect. For a first introduction to this idea see: Stein, 1955.

** This work has been published at a conference. See: Kaptein, 2011.

Professor called BJ Fogg who we have already met in Chapter 2. BJ was one of the first people to foresee the use of persuasion by computers and is the author of an influential book on Persuasive Technologies.

Before Dean and I met, BJ had already thought about what he called 'persuasion profiles'. These persuasion profiles would describe which types of influence strategies individuals were susceptible to. At that time BJ and his students created a short video demonstration of the use of these persuasion profiles in interactive media. This video had never been formally published, so I was unaware of its existence. But Dean did know of it, since he himself had studied under BJ Fogg. When I watched the video I saw that after my very long journey of investigating the effects of persuasion principles, the effects of stacking, and the individual differences in the effects of persuasion, I had arrived at a thought that was already demonstrated in a video that was several years old!

It is about time I explained what exactly a persuasion profile is. Although BJ already visualized the consequences of the persuasion profiles in a video, it was unclear from the video how these profiles would be built and used. This however is what I will try to explain next. And during this explanation I hope that you will see that persuasion profiles are distinct from other profiles that are often used in marketing.

Formally, a persuasion profile is 'A collection of the estimates of the effect of persuasion principles (and the certainty of these estimates) for an individual.' Figure 4 shows my personal persuasion profile.

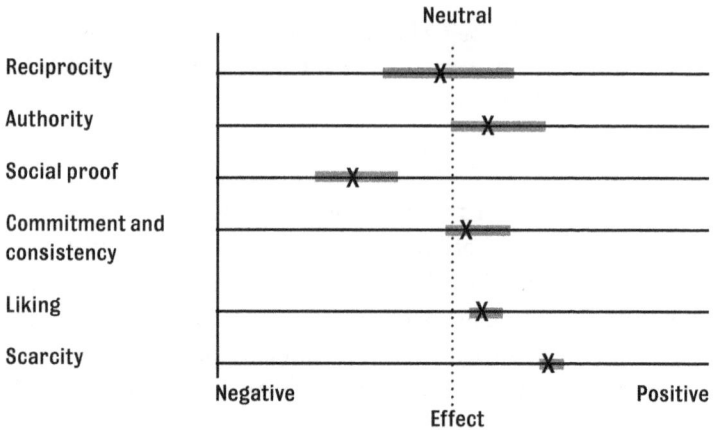

Figure 4: Influencing my own profile. On the y -axis the six interference principles are represented. The x- axis shows the estimate of the effect of each of these principles for me personally. The effect of social proof to me is quite limited and is even counter-productive (smaller than 0). The effects of scarcity and author-ity are in contrast strongly positive.

It is clear from this profile that I am not very susceptible to social proof: apparently I am not very swayed by the opinions of others. Actually, you can see that the effect of this principle is negative: social proof messages are less effective than messages that do not explicitly use persuasion. The scarcity and the authority principles however do work well for me: both estimates are clearly positive. If you want to influence me these would be a good choice.

Besides these estimates the profile also shows the certainty of the estimates. It is clear that for me the estimate for the effect of the reciprocity principle is fairly uncertain. This is indicated by the large horizontal bar surrounding it. It is logical that in practice the estimates of those principles that we believe to be ineffective are uncertain: why would we try to get a lot of observations for the effect of an influence attempt that is likely unsuccessful?

Figure 5 shows how my profile changes over time; for example as I browse an online store that uses different persuasive principles to sell me products. Every time I see a product and click on it or add it to my shopping cart my profile can be adjusted. A click on the product counts as a success for the principle that was used to pitch that product and the profile can be updated by counting the number of successes. As I roam the Internet, and as more and more of my responses to influence attempts become available, my profile becomes more informed. And as the persuasion profile grows more accurate and more confident, it can be used to make a better choice. This is exactly the way in which machines can learn which types of persuasion work. By using persuasion profiles, machines can become like offline sellers: they can slowly but surely zoom in on the right sales arguments that persuade one to buy a product. Using persuasion profiles, online stores can thus increase their impact.

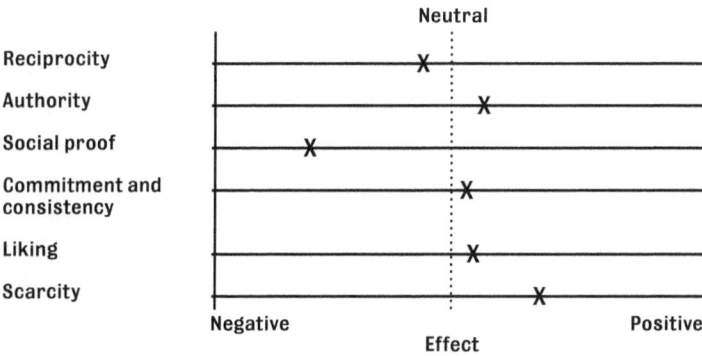

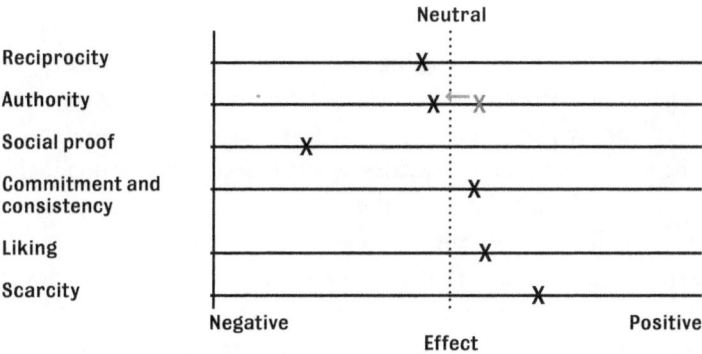

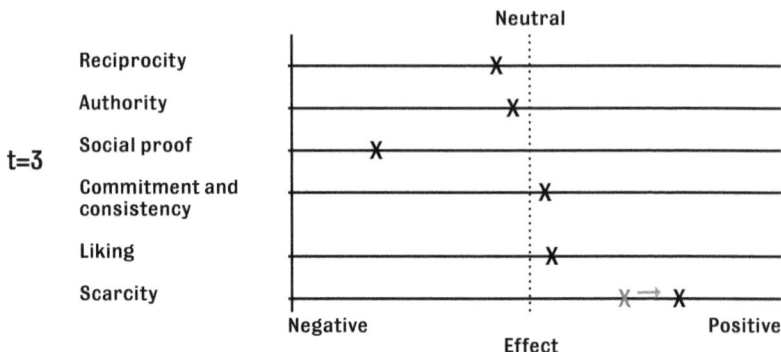

Figure 5: The evolution of a persuasion profile over time. As certain principles prove to be successful, the estimate of their success changes. Here we see that the principle of Authority is not successful, while the Scarcity principle is.

Your profile is probably different from mine, and that of your neighbor might be different still. Since we all have a unique persuasion profile, these profiles are not like the profiles we know about in traditional marketing: persuasion profiles do not identify four types of people, but rather there are as many profiles as there are people. The only thing that the computer does, by using the profile, is learn from previous interactions with you and make an informed choice about the next persuasion principle to be used. This profile can be used to decide for you personally which message should be shown on the sign in front of the Marriott to persuade you to use the revolving door. Since it describes what types of persuasion work for you, this exact same profile can also be used to effectively pitch a book to you when you enter an online store. The persuasion profile describes how to best persuade individuals.

The above description of the persuasion profile might seem a bit complicated and raise questions: do we really need to track everyone and change the profiles all the time to increase impact online? And, is it not a bit scary if we are storing a profile of your personal weaknesses somewhere on a central server,? Practically speaking, however, it is not at all hard to keep these profiles on a

server and this is why I believe this will be more and more common in the future. To apply and use persuasion profiles only three
simple requirements need to be met, each of which is obvious in
the revolving door example.

First, we need to have messages that use different persuasion
principles. In the revolving door example we looked at three different messages, each implementing a different persuasion principle. Second, we need to be able to identify individuals. Since
the persuasion profile is unique to individuals we must be able to
keep track of who we are interacting with. In the revolving door
example I discussed face recognition or the Bluetooth key of a mobile phone as a means of identification. However, there are many
other possibilities for tracking individuals. The last ingredient for
creating a persuasion profile is a method of measuring the effect of
the attempt to influence. In the revolving door example this was
easy: we were able to use the same tracking that we used to identify
individuals to see which door they took. If the visitor took the
revolving door, the persuasion principle was a success, and if they
took the sliding door it was a failure. In different situations the
measure of success might not always be so trivial; once it's possible
to display different messages to people, to identify people, and to
measure the effect of the messages, then we can make a persuasion
profile.

EXPLORE NEW PRINCIPLES OR EXPLOIT THE KNOWLEDGE THAT YOU HAVE

There is something that I have not yet put forward when discussing how persuasion profiles can be used to select the best message
for each individual. I told you that if the social proof message had
the highest estimate, then that is the one we should select. However, this is an over-simplification. While this book contains many
simplifications – it is after all not a scientific article – the current
simplification begs extra attention. I feel obliged to explain in a bit
more depth how we can use the estimates contained in the persuasion profile to select messages. The story will be a bit technical so I
will try to introduce it using a simple example.

Suppose you have 1,000 USD at your disposal and you are fac-

ing four slot machines. Further suppose that you know the owner
of the slot machines and he has told you that one of the machines
is more successful than the others: one of the machines will allow
you to win more often.

Let's also imagine that these are very simple slot machines: you
put in a dollar, press the button, and you either win or lose. If you
win, you always win the same amount: 10$. So, the more success-
ful machine does nothing more than giving you wins more often
than the others. For example, one slot machine will give you a
win eighty out of a thousand plays (8 percent), while the other
three only forty out of a thousand plays (4 percent). The problem
however is you do not know which of the four slot machines is the
successful machine. You know one of them pays out more, but you
have no clue which one. *

I hope you recognize the analogy of selecting the correct persuasion principle for an individual: we know one of the principles
will be most effective. However we do not know which one. There
is a limited set of options available – the slot machines or the persuasive principles – and our aim is to find out which of the options
is most successful.

The problem we are facing is easy to state but hard to answer:
how are we going to find out which of the options is most successful? Or, more accurately, the question should really be: how
are we going to make as much money as possible playing the slot
machines that stand before us despite the fact that we do not know
which one is most effective before playing it?

For your first throw you really have nothing to go on. At that
time all slots are equal since you have no idea which one will be
better or worse. So, perhaps you throw your first dollar in the leftmost slot. You insert the dollar, press the button, see the reels spin-
ning, and 'hooray': you just made 10 dollars!

That was not too bad. You had immediate success. However,

---

* You might have computed that 80 × 10 is 800$ and thus, in the long run,
you will lose money. This is often true: in casinos you will lose money in the
long run. The best strategy – in reality when talking about slot machines – is
not to throw in your money at all.

what do you do with your second dollar? You basically have two options: you can choose the leftmost slot again, since it seemed to be effective, or you can randomly choose one of the other slots. Choosing the leftmost slot would mean that you exploit the rather limited knowledge that you have based on the first play: the leftmost machine pays off. Choosing one of the new slots however would mean exploring your options. This gives you the opportunity to learn about the effect of the other machines. If you never throw a dollar into the other machines, you will never be able to learn anything about them.

In science this dilemma is called the 'explore-exploit trade-off'. This trade-off is omnipresent in dynamic learning systems – of which you, facing the slot machines, are part of. Choosing the left-most machine again when playing your second dollar means exploiting the knowledge you have, while choosing another machine means exploring the possibilities. The two actions cannot be done at once: each time you need to decide whether you will spend money on exploring your options or whether you will exploit your current knowledge.

A very common strategy for solving the problem of how to minimize my search cost and make sure that I play the most successful slot as often as possible is the following: you throw 100 of your 1,000 dollars into each of the four machines and observe the results. Let's say they look like this:

- Machine 1 (left): 3 wins out of 100 tries
- Machine 2: 6 wins out of 100 tries
- Machine 3: 8 wins out of 100 tries
- Machine 4: 4 wins out of 100 tries

So far you have not yet been using any of the knowledge you had; you only played the slots to learn about them. After this exploration period you make a decision: you choose the highest scoring machine and throw in the remaining 600 dollars. In this case, you would end up selecting machine number 3.

This is exactly what we do when we perform A/B tests or multivariate tests when we try to optimize websites (see Chapter 4).

For example, if we have four distinct persuasion principles that we can use to offer a product, we can test each of these for a while. We could for example expose 10,000 customers to each of the principles. After running this test, we can see which version had the highest conversion rate, and we can select that version for future use.

But, what would you think if I told you that in the case of our four slot machines, in reality, machine two is the one that has a win probability of 8 percent? The others all have a probability of four percent. You just happened to be lucky this time playing machine number 3. This will have a major implication for the exploiting period that follows the experiment. Your expected pay-off playing the machine of your choosing with your remaining 600 dollars is .04 × 600 × 10 = 240 dollars. If you had correctly chosen machine number two however, your pay off would have been a whopping .08 × 600 × 10 = 480 dollars.

It should be clear from this example that moving too quickly into exploitation when you are not yet certain of your choice is not a good idea. However, selecting a very long exploration period will also not do you much good: you will end up playing the unsuccessful machines too often to learn about them. The exact length of the observation period however cannot be determined if you do not know the pay off probabilities of the slot machines. *

HOW TO SPEND YOUR MONEY ON THE SLOT MACHINES

Mathematicians have studied the slot machine problem for years. And the good news is that they have an optimal solution in the case of two slots: in that specific case it is possible to precisely figure out how you should distribute your money. The bad news however is that once the numbers of slot machines increase, things get very very difficult. To be honest, even the two machine version is difficult. For general explore-exploit problems there is no solution that is guaranteed to work best.

---

* The tests of statistical significance that most of us have heard of really are a very bad decision criterion for deciding in the above situation.

Fortunately however there is a relatively simple way of distributing your money that will always outperform the fixed exploration period followed by an exploitation period. Therefore, we can easily do better than the A/B test. A very successful way of allocating your money is as follows: for each slot machine you estimate the probability of success and you maintain an estimate of your certainty of that estimate. In the beginning you will be very uncertain since you have very little information. The estimation of the success probability and its certainty can be done in the same way I described for the revolving door, using a probability distribution.

When you start spending your money, you look at your estimates and their certainty. Thus you have four different probability distributions, one for each machine. These look something like this if you don't know anything to the contrary: Machine one has a 25% chance of winning, machine 2 has a 25% chance of winning, machine three 25%, and machine four 25%. These are your first estimates and are very uncertain. Now you proceed as follows:

1. You randomly choose a slot (each slot has a 1 in 4 chance of being selected).
2. You throw your dollar in the selected slot and check the result.
3. Based on the results, you determine a new probability distribution for the machine that you have just played. For example, you threw your dollar in slot two and you got lucky: the slot machine pays 10 dollars. The update of your distribution now is easy: instead of an initial estimate of success of 1 in 4, your new estimate for machine two is now 2 (the first success that you had, plus the success of the additional dollar) in 5 (4 + 1). So your new estimate will be 40%.
4. Your next choice will not now be uniformly random, as in step one, in which each machine had an equal probability of being played; but rather you will base the probabilities of playing the machines on your observation of machine two. Because machine two was successful, you do not select it

with a probability of ¼, but with a slightly higher probability, say 2/5.*

5. You indefinitely repeat steps 2 through 4. Each time you adjust the probability distribution that you have in your head for the machine that you played in that round. And, every following round you change the probabilities of selecting the machines.

Because the probability of selecting a machine depends on the success of the machine and your certainty around your estimate of the success (e.g. the number of times you explored that machine), you will occasionally play machines which you think are unsuccessful but of which you are uncertain. However, you will more often play those machines that pay off more. And, as you get more and more certain, the probability that your money is going into the best machine steadily increases. In the long run this way of playing the machines gives you an optimal result.**

The method of playing the slot machines that you have just read is called 'randomized probably matching'. I tried to make the explanation intuitive by omitting some of the details. I hope you have at least managed to distill the following: if you have a persuasion profile of a person which includes estimates of the effects of persuasion principles and their certainty, you can use this profile to select messages. By continuously alternating between exploring new principles and exploiting observations that you have, you can maximize the effect of the messages that you are displaying to people. Every time you display a message containing a persuasive principle you can improve your estimates by those responses. In this way it is possible to dynamically create a persuasion profile.

---

* You now arrive at the following estimates: 1/4, 2/5, 1/4 and 1/4. To transform these into a legitimate probability distribution it needs to be rescaled to sum to one: 5/23, 8/23, 5/23 and 5/23. These probabilities can then be used to select the slot machine for the next play. In real applications, often a Bayesian specification of the problem is used, complicating it a bit (and leading to different estimates). However, I hope the example gives some intuition.
** See: Scott, 2010.

This dynamically built persuasion profile closely mimics the be-havior of good salesperson: it allows us to zoom in on the right argument for the right person. However, by using the persuasive principles as introduced by Cialdini in combination with dynamic learning, we can have a computer do the job, which really increas-es the impact of our online communication!

The persuasion profile assures us that every response you as a customer provide to interactive messages allows us to learn about your psychological makeup. Slowly but surely, while you browse the web, the computer gets to know which psychological persua-sion principles work for you. However, before we discuss whether this is desirable, we will first see whether or not it actually works in practice.

SUMMARIZING

The previous chapters have shown that persuasion principles can heavily influence the impact of digital technologies. However, we also saw that not all of these persuasion principles should be ap-plied at once. Given the large differences between individuals in their responses to persuasion principles we should personalize our selection of persuasive messages. In this chapter I have tried to explain how persuasion profiles can be used to select messages for individuals. The main take-aways are:

- A persuasion profile is a collection of estimates of the effects of distinct persuasion principles for an individual – and the certainty around those estimates.
- A persuasion profile can be based on questionnaires or (bet-ter yet) on the actual behavior of people. Every time a res-ponse to a persuasion principle is observed, the persuasion profile can be improved.
- By using randomized probability matching, a smart way to address the explore-exploit trade-off, the persuasion profile can be used effectively while learning.
- In the next chapter, I will show how this works in practice...

10

PERSUASION PROFILES IN PRACTICE

Rosa and I are in a shoe store right next to my favorite bookstore. Admittedly, I do not particularly like this store. However, Rosa loves it and frequents it. She visits the store regularly enough to notice when they have new shoes in stock. The salesmen in the shoe store are however less well trained – or just less experienced – than the vendors in the bookstore. They hardly recognize Rosa. To them, she is a new customer every time.

While visiting this time, a young woman heads our way. She appears to be a saleswomen and she walks directly towards Rosa. Rosa is holding a rather ugly shoe. 'Those are doing very well this season! They are the new trend for the summer.' The saleswoman nailed the right argument for Rosa. The shoe that she is looking at is approved by the masses. What more could one wish for?

The saleswomen in the above example just happened to have hit the right message for Rosa. For me, she would have missed it completely. She might have known about the persuasion principles as introduced by Cialdini, but it seems she was using the exact same argument for everyone. In the previous chapter we discussed how personalization could overcome the possible adverse effects of selecting the wrong persuasion principles. We also discussed how persuasion profiles can be used by computers to automate this task and personalize persuasion even in computer-to-human interactions. However, we have discussed it in theory only.

If you are even mildly skeptical you will need a bit more convincing before you believe that persuasion profiles increase the impact of digital communication. This is exactly what I will try to do in this Chapter. We will discuss three successful examples of the use of persuasion profiles to increase impact. And, finally, I will try to explain how you yourself, if you are in the influencing business, can use persuasion online.

EXAMPLES OF PERSUASION PROFILES IN PRACTICE

Actually, we have already discussed quite a lot of indirect evidence in favor of the effects of persuasion profiles on the impact of digital communication. Dean Eckles and I showed that estimates of the effect of persuasion at the individual level better explain responses than do aggregate level summaries. We showed that a person's previous response to a persuasion principle was more predictive of a future response than the responses of other – possibly similar – people. This is the result that opened the door to the personalization of persuasion principles. I also showed that questionnaires that query people's susceptibility to persuasion can help increase impact. Those who appeared to be susceptible to social proof arguments indeed complied more when an implementation of the social proof principle was used, and those who appeared to be susceptible to authority arguments indeed were more swayed by implementations of that principle. Boris de Ruyter and I even managed to use the scores on a susceptibility questionnaire to increase the effect of text messages created to reduce people's snacking. We showed that in this case personalized persuasion was more effective than other ways of selecting persuasive messages.

Still, all of these studies provided one-shot examples, and all of them were experimental: none was done in a real persuasive context. You are probably inclined to believe that in a well-conducted study, in which all other factors are controlled for, personalized persuasion can make a difference and increase impact. However, in practice it will be hard to obtain questionnaire scores. Also, it will be hard to control the environment in full. Thus, we need to find evidence of the effect of persuasion profiles based on direct behavioral measurements in 'the wild': when people actually respond in real life instead of when they are participating in a study.

In this Chapter I will provide some evidence of the effect of persuasion profiles on the impact of interactive communication in the wild.

Example 1: Take the stairs

After discussing the revolving door with both Abhay and Dean I decided to actually build such a system. At that time I was working at the Technical University of Eindhoven in the Netherlands and I was teaching a course in a post-master User-System Interaction program. Together with a group of students who were enrolled in the course I tried to gather some of the first evidence of the effect of persuasion profiles in the wild.

Ryo, Sarah, Peter, and Leoni had just started a joint design project that was part of the program. Within their design project, they wanted to create an interactive technology aimed at influencing the behavior of its users. At the time I was one of the specialists in this field working for the Eindhoven University of Technology and I was asked to coach their design project. They were a group of highly motivated and intelligent students and all had experience in building interactive systems. So I wondered whether building the revolving door systems would be of interest in completing their design project.

However, Ryo, Sarah, Peter, and Leoni had different interests. They primarily saw the potential of interactive technologies as motivating people to lead a healthier lifestyle: an application of persuasive technologies that many researchers work on. Specifically, the students wanted to motivate people to work out more and lead a less sedentary life. Leading a healthy life style and working out more are often much harder to measure than using a revolving door. Furthermore, whether or not you work out – for example go for a run – will depend not only on the interactive technology that supports it, but also on many other contextual factors such as the weather. These contextual factors and the challenges in measuring the success of attempts to influence in this setting made it less than an ideal candidate for testing the effect of persuasion profiles.

However, the students came up with an idea in which the goals of testing persuasion profiles in the wild and motivating people to lead a less sedentary life could be combined. It was this: If we can motivate people to take the stairs instead of the elevator to the floor on which they work, they will be more active. Quite a lot of research has been done on the effects of taking the stairs – increasing the moderately intensive activities of people during the day. Actually, taking the stairs a few times a day alone means that you almost hit the recommended daily level of moderate physical activity, especially if you work on the fourth floor or higher. Hence, motivating people to take the stairs instead of the elevator could have a significant impact on their health.

At the time we were all working in a building with a fairly long hallway that led up to both the stairs and the elevators. This hallway gave us the opportunity – similar to the revolving door scenario – to display messages to workers entering the building. In these messages we could use different persuasion principles. We could therefore motivate people to lead a healthier lifestyle – or at least take the stairs. If we could also identify workers, we would be able to track the effect of our influence attempt. It would not be too hard to identify workers both when they entered the building as well as when they entered either the elevator or the stairs. This gave us all the ingredients we needed to build our interactive system: we were able to identify people, produce different messages each implementing distinct persuasion principles, and we could directly observe the effect.

We started with the design of different messages. We first wanted to make sure that messages displayed on a screen in the hallway would have an effect on the people entering the office building. We knew, of course, that on average the principles identified by Cialdini would have a positive effect, but we wanted to make sure that the messages worked in this novel situation. For the first few days, we placed a screen in the hallway that stated: 'Take the stairs!' This was the ultimate goal of our system, and we kept track of the proportion of people entering the building who took the stairs. We then expanded our set of messages. We added messages such as:

- '90 percent of your colleagues take the stairs' (social proof)
- 'Fitness instructors encourage you to take the stairs' (authority)

or

- 'Today is a good day to take the stairs!' (scarcity)

We also measured the effect of these messages for a number of days. And, not surprisingly, Cialdini was right: we were able to show that on average more people took the stairs when persuasion principles were added to the messages.

However, after assuring ourselves that persuasive messages could really make a difference in our situation, we had to face the technical challenge of identifying and tracking workers. We wanted to identify workers without letting them know what we were doing. We did not want people to identify themselves, but rather we wanted to do the identification unobtrusively. We needed to identify workers to personalize the messages. In theory there are quite a number of technologies available that would allow us to recognize people. Facial recognition, for example, is fairly well developed. However, we tried a number of off-the-shelf solutions for facial recognition but it turned out that it was really hard to identify people properly as they entered the hallway. The solution works very well if someone looks directly into a camera, but when someone is just walking by it's much harder to get it right.

Following research by Kostakos (2008),* we tried, to find out whether or not we could use the Bluetooth key of mobile devices that people carried to recognize them. We found that by continuously scanning the Bluetooth device ID in the hallway, we were able to uniquely identify about 8% of the workers that entered the hallway. These workers apparently carried a device that emitted an identifiable signal, and this signal enabled us to identify them uniquely for many days and in many locations. Although we were only able to track a selection of office workers, we did have a means of identifying people.

Now that we were able to identify people, it was also easy to measure the effect of our messages: we could easily track whether a person was identified when entering the hallway when the person

---

* See for details: Kostakos, 2008.

walked past the screen with the message. And, finally, we could track, using a Bluetooth scanner both in the elevator as well as in the staircase, whether or not the message was successful. We now had all the technology in place to directly test the revolving door scenario. However, we had changed the purpose of the attempt from one aimed at reducing energy consumption to one that motivated people to work out more: exactly the aim that Ryo, Sarah, Peter, and Leoni were interested in.

We set up a full interactive system, including a fast central server that would carry out the calculations needed to decide which message to show to which worker. But we did not just turn the system on: we actually wanted to know whether this use of persuasion profiles was more effective than the general use of persuasive principles. Accordingly, we decided that we would use a persuasion profile to select messages for only half of the workers entering the hallway. For the other half of the visitors a random selection of the messages was made.

The system was in operation for about two months in our building. Workers would come in and they would be recognized. Then we would give them a persuasive message. Finally, we recorded the effect: did the worker take the stairs?

After two months, there were actually only 34 workers that we had seen more than once, but regretfully we had to dismantle our system (by higher order). So, it was time for us to look at our data.

Initially we inspected the data at the level of individuals: were we able to show that returning visitors were more inclined to take the stairs than first time visitors? Did the impact of the messages increase? We saw that we were able to keep and build a profile which, as expected, became more and more certain over time: thus we would be able to make more informed decisions over time. For the limited number of people that we were able to recognize regularly, we indeed saw that the persuasion profiles made the messages more and more successful over time. This, in our view, was the first real-life demonstration of the use of persuasion profiles.

We obviously also wanted to see whether we outperformed the randomly selected messages. To do so we compared the average tendency to take the stairs in both groups and we found that the group for which persuasion profiles were used took the stairs more often. However, due to the limited number of people we were able to identify, our estimates of the success of both methods were very uncertain. And because of our uncertainty we were unable to make a definite decision in favor of persuasion profiles. Thus, we had created the first system that used persuasion profiles in the wild, and we had some indications of its success, but we were unable to show a convincing difference in favor of persuasion profiles.

We revealed these results at a conference a few months later and the audience was impressed by the system and our technological abilities. They agreed that the results were promising. However, they were also skeptical – as they should be. Because of the limited number of observations we had been able to collect, hardly anyone was willing to accept the fact that persuasion profiles really worked. We could have just been lucky with our specific workers.[*]

EXAMPLE 2: THE EFFECTIVENESS OF REMINDER EMAILS
After presenting the persuasive system designed to motivate people to take the stairs, I began searching for different situations in which I could show the impact of persuasion profiles. I had to find another situation in which we could use the different persuasive principles and measure their effect. And, obviously it had to be possible to identify people and follow them for a while. I was really looking for a situation in which I could identify everyone, not just the 8% we managed to track using Bluetooth.

During that time I was also working on an industrial research project. For that project we had access to some great new technology: we had access to an activity monitor. The activity monitor was a very small device – waterproof – that could measure at each point in time whether or not users were seated, whether they were biking, walking, or running, or whether they were swimming. We were experimenting with different types of feedback that would encourage users to be more active.

We had access to thousands of people who used the activity monitor daily. However, to make their personal data available,

_____
[*] For the full article see: Sakai, Peteghem, Sande, Banach & Kaptein, 2011.

users had to connect their activity monitors to their computers using a physical wire. Unfortunately, quite a few of the users would occasionally forget to upload their data. If we did not have access to their activity data, we were unable to provide relevant feedback or coaching. Even more worrying was the fact that if people forgot to upload their data for a number of weeks, they often stopped using the device completely and they dropped out of the coaching program. The moment that happened, the product failed in its goal since the user would not become more active. So, to encourage users to keep uploading their data we would regularly send them reminder emails.

While I was working on this project, I was thinking about a new situation in which to test persuasion profiles simultaneously. I think it took more than a month before I actually combined the two. We could use the reminder emails of the activity-coaching program to test persuasion profiles! Perhaps we could increase the effectiveness of the reminder emails by personalizing the persuasive messages that we used.

This time, I wanted to be very sure that we could obtain results that would be convincing enough. We needed to have enough data available – enough people who received multiple reminder emails – to prove the effect of persuasion profiles. So I decided to look at our current logs: I was able to see that there were quite a few people – definitely sufficient – who had received multiple reminder emails pver a few months. Also, it was clear that the reminder emails often had an effect: quite a number of users who received the reminder emails would upload their data shortly afterwards.

Together with Aart van Halteren, the leader of the research team that developed the activity monitor, I figured out a way to test the impact of persuasion profiles using the reminder emails. We started by making many versions of the reminder emails, each with different implementations of persuasive principles. We ended up adding relatively short sentences to the original emails. Sentences like: 'Thousands of people actively participate in the program' or 'Today is your opportunity to learn about your activity'.

In addition to rewriting the email reminders we also added a small dynamic image to each of the emails. These dynamic emails allowed us to see whether or not users had opened them. This gave us all the data we needed: we could send out an email with different persuasive principles. We could then measure whether or not people had looked at the emails. Finally, we could link the email open-rate with the data uploads from the activity monitors to see whether or not the emails were a success. If users uploaded their activity to our central servers within several hours of opening the email, this would be counted as a success increasing the estimate of the principle that was used in the email in the users' persuasion profiles. Vice versa if the user did not upload the activity after reading the email; the effectiveness would be reduced. This allowed us, over time, to build and use a persuasion profile.

The final experiment we conducted was slightly more complex than the previous one. This time we divided the users into four groups to estimate the effects of persuasion profiles:

1. The 'Baseline' group: This group of users continued to receive the same e-mail reminders they had always gotten. For these people nothing changed.
2. The 'Best tested' group: Before we started our experiment we asked eighty people to judge the messages we created and asked them: which of these messages was most persuasive. The users who were assigned to the Best-tested group received the message that was deemed most persuasive based on this pre-test.
3. The 'Random' group: This group of users would receive a randomly selected message from all the messages we created each time a reminder email was send.
4. The 'Persuasion profiling' group: For this group of users we maintained a persuasion profile which we updated dynamically. Thus, over time we zoomed in on the best persuasive principles for those users.

Of course we were hoping that the impact of the messages would be highest in group number four.

Aart and I let this field experiment run for six months. During that
time the different groups each received their own messages. Eventually we had 1,129 users who, during the trial period, received at
least three reminder emails. We used the data from this selection
of users to examine the differences between the four groups.

This time the difference between the persuasion profiling
group and the other groups was clear and convincing. Aart and I
found that the messages – in all of the groups – became less and
less successful over time. This is not very strange: since some people completely drop out of the program after a while but still open
the emails. We expected that the effect of the reminders would decrease over time. But we also found large differences between the
different groups in the speed at which the effectiveness decreased.

In the Best-tested group the emails became largely ineffective
very quickly.* This group was closely followed by the Baseline
group and the Random group. The clear winner – in the sense
that the emails remained effective the longest – was the Persuasion
profiling group. After only five reminders, the emails in this group
were 20% more effective than those in the random group. And the
more reminders were sent, the greater the difference between the
groups became.

Aart and I not only looked at the success of the individual
reminders, but we also looked at the drop-out rate. We studied
how many people totally stopped uploading their data for each
group in the experiment. Here the same pattern was clear: in the
Best-tested group drop-out rates were very high. And again the
Persuasion profiling groups had the best score: the drop-out rate
in that group during the experiment was the lowest of all. The difference in drop-out rates was almost 25 percent! That is a huge difference. Perhaps you have not yet been convinced by the power of
persuasion profiles, but for me this experiment clearly showed how
persuasion profiles can increase the impact of interactive communication.

---

* To me this highlights the fact that people are unable to judge which
messages will persuade them. This strengthens my own belief that behavior
(operative) measures are much more useful than questionnaire measures.

Although Aart and I were very excited about our findings, we did not actually end up including them in the commercial version of the product. This was easily explained: during the experiment the initial studies that Dean Eckles and I carried out were featured in a number of popular media. However, the work was not always featured positively: Some of the articles had titles like 'Insider trading' and 'Welcome to the brave new world of Persuasion Profiling'.* In some of these articles the idea of persuasion profiling was regarded as manipulation, which had a very different connotation compared to persuasion or seduction. The managers of the product did not really like this kind of language being associated with a product intended to make users more active, and hence they decided not to include persuasion profiling.

While this seems reasonable from a reputational stance, I did not agree with the decision. Since the aim of the product is to make people healthier I believed that the company should do all in its power to make the product work for everyone. Clearly, the product had a larger effect when persuasion profiling was used in the reminder emails than when it was not. This means that the final commercial product – in my opinion – was less successful than it could have been. However, we will discuss some of these concerns in the next Chapter. Let's first look at another example of the use of persuasion profiles.**

Example 3: Persuasion Profiles in e-commerce

The one example we have not yet discussed is the application of persuasion profiles in e-commerce. I actually started this book talking about the differences between online and offline stores, and it is about time that we saw whether or not persuasion profiles actually increase the effect of online stores.

Quite coincidentally, I had the opportunity to test the use of persuasion profiles in an online store. About six years ago, Mau-

---

* See: http://www.wired.com/magazine/2011/04/st_essay_persuasion_profiling/
** For the full description of the reminder email study see: Kaptein & Van Halteren, 2012.

rice de Kunder, one of the best programmers that I know, inspired me to start my own online store. Maurice himself was and still is very successful with his own online business. He, like no one else that I know, is able to make sure that the pages that he builds rank high in search engines. By subsequently adding advertisements to these high-ranking – and thus high traffic – pages he is able to make a very decent living. At that time I wanted to be like him: I wanted to make money with my own webpage that scored high on Google. I started an online store for children's clothing. Within a few days I managed to build an online store and within two weeks I had hit Google's first page when searching for 'children's clothing'. And, I actually made some money.*

After about four weeks I lost interest in the website. Every month I would make a small sum of money, but I did not have the motivation or the knowledge to develop the store. A few years later however, when I became interested in persuasion profiles, and the store drew in a few hundred visitors a month it proved to be a good testing ground for persuasion profiles.

The clothing website was very simple: on the front page it displayed a random selection of products in a number of small tiles including the best-selling products and the special offers. The site offered a number of categories to browse through, and it offered a search function. The product page itself consisted of a large picture of the product and a textual description. Just below the products there was a link to purchase the product.

At the precise time I was creating the website, I was busily studying online persuasion. I had already used a number of persuasion principles and it did not prove very hard to add a few more. I changed the email codes that I used on the children's clothing website, and within a few days I was able to make persuasion profiles of each of the visitors to the website. I created labels that said 'special offer' or 'bestseller' and I was able to toggle these on or off depending on the persuasion profile.

---

* The store was an 'affiliate store'. Hence, I did not have any clothing to sell myself, but rather forwarded visitors to online stores that would actually have the products in stock.

The actual logic of which label to show was hosted on a separate server. That server stored the persuasion profiles for each visitor, and it stored whether or not the product page was a success. Based on this information the profiles could be updated, and for each page view it was possible to decide what message to show. It took a few tweaks in the code to make the persuasion profile run in real-time. With the email study we had quite a bit of time to compute our estimates, but this time I wanted to update the page between page-views. I managed to get it all up and running.

After several months of development and testing, the whole system seemed to work well: it was fast, and it could track every visitor. I used the two labels and the possibility of not showing a label at all as the three possible messages for each product. In addition, as in the previous evaluations, I added a control group: for half of the visitors only the default version of the product page would be shown and no persuasion profile would be created. For four months I tracked every customer after which I decided to look at the data collected.

First, I compared the impact of persuasion profiles with the default version of the website. I examined the daily performance of the site. In the first few days, the differences between the baseline version and the persuasion profiling version were minor. However, it was soon clear that the version that used persuasion profiles had a greater impact than the original version of the page. The number of clicks on products was significantly higher: I achieved an increase of about 20 percent. And, the actual sales were also higher. The persuasion profiles indeed increased the impact of the page, and in doing so increased the overall effect of the store.

Figure 6 shows in detail the effect of the use of persuasion profiles. The Figure shows the probability of a customer buying a product as a function of the number of products that he or she views. The more pages the customer views, the more likely they are to buy a product. So, the impact of the website increases as the number of page-views increases. This makes sense: if you are looking at many different products you probably intend to buy something and eventually do buy a product – when you find what you are

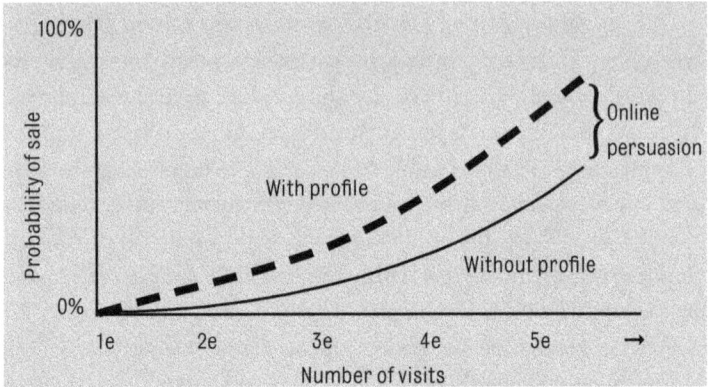

Figure 6: The estimated probability (y – axis) that a customer will buy a product as a function of the number of times that the customer visits the page (x – axis). When using persuasion profiles the success probability increases faster without the profiles.

looking for. However, the two separate graph lines show clearly the difference between the use of persuasion profiles and the default version of the online store: the probability of a sale increases much faster when persuasion profiles are used. As an increasingly better choice of persuasion principles is made, the online store that uses persuasion profiles also becomes increasingly more effective.*

Finally, I also examined the results for individual customers. I could see the persuasion profiles evolve, and for each visitor – especially those who visited a number of pages – I could see which persuasion principle was most effective. I was able to see that products that were pitched using a persuasion principle were sold more often than those that were pitched without active persuasion. Again I replicated the findings Cialdini had demonstrated. And, I could clearly see that some visitors found one strategy more appealing, while others seemed more attracted by the other strategy: this replicated the results that Dean and I had found in our earlier studies.

---

* This study can be found in: Kaptein & Parvinen, 2012.

USING PERSUASION ONLINE

We have just seen three examples of the impact of persuasion profiles in the wild. In each case the profiles were created based on the behavior of people, not on questionnaire measures. The examples all show an increase in impact with the use of persuasion profiles. The use of personalized persuasion can have a considerable effect on people's decisions: whether these concern a response to an email, the purchase of a product, or the decision to take the stairs.

I assume that by now you are convinced of the use of persuasion profiles to increase the impact and eventually the effect of digital communication. I have described three applications and I have detailed the results of the use of persuasion profiles in each of them. However, I have not really told you how you can start using persuasion effectively yourself to persuade others online. What can you start doing tomorrow to make your online business more effective?

There are many possible answers to the above question. As you might have read in the description on the back of this book, I am the founder of a company called Science Rockstars which markets PersuasionAPI.* This company sells the ability to create, maintain, and use persuasion profiles. We tackle the algorithm side of things, and we offer it as a service. However, PersuasionAPI is certainly not the only product or company in this market. More and more companies are offering their skills to personalize online content. So, one possible way of getting started with persuasion profiles in your online communication is to get an external party to help you make it work.

Actually, external parties are not a necessity at all. What I would really recommend is that you start experimenting first; and remember to start small. A few simple changes to your online sales process are likely to increase the effect of your online communication efforts. I will try to explain how you can, without tricky algorithms, improve the impact of your communication. The information in this book is enough to get you started. I will try to

---

* You can find the company at www.sciencerockstars.com. At www.persuasionapi.com you can see how we build persuasion profiles.

explain the first steps using an example.

About two years ago I received an email from Drew Gillson who was the manager of the Canadian website www.liveoutthere.com at that time. The website sells, outdoor clothing and equipment. Drew, by coincidence, had read one of my scientific papers on persuasion profiling and decided to experiment with some of the ideas on his own website. In his email, Drew enthusiastically explained how he increased the impact of the store by just making some minor changes.

What Drew did was pretty simple. The number of articles sold on the site was huge – there were jackets, shoes, and so on. Some of the messages on his front page – which seem to have been changed since the last time I checked – used to feature a message stating 'Our employees' favorite'. In other words these were the products that the team of liveoutthere.com recommended. You obviously recognize this as an implementation of the authority principle.

Although Drew had been using these little labels long before he had read the article, it did get him thinking. There might be many different reasons someone clicks on a jacket that is recommended by the staff,. One obvious reason is that the jacket itself appeals to the customer. But it could also be true that the customer favors the authority principle.

On the next product page, however, the customer was only able to see that jacket, and more jackets of that kind. So, now the only possible reason for clicking was the appeal of the product itself. There was no list of other items that were recommended by the staff.

After reading the article Drew decided to add this list. He did not use complicated algorithms or dynamic profiles. The only thing he did was make sure that after a consumer clicked on a product that was recommended by the staff, the following page featured a list of other products recommended by the staff. And, this very minor change to the online store increased its impact. The addition of the recommended items list had indeed increased the conversion rates for the store!

Getting started with persuasion profiles

Drew's example shows how an authority argument,. the selection made by the staff, can be used on a website. Drew not only presented the argument, but also ensured that visitors who appeared to appreciate the argument were shown it more often. It is fairly simple to imitate Drew's implementation using the following steps:

1. You create implementations of the principles proposed by Cialdini. Here you should use an implementation not only of the principle of authority – as Drew did – but also of the other principles. We have already encountered quite a few examples of implementations of social proof, authority, and scarcity in this Chapter. For more guidance please see the suggested implementations in Table 3.
2. You use a selection of the messages you created one by one! (on your website or in your emails) You can, for example, display a list of special offers on your front page (scarcity), or send an email promoting your bestselling products (social proof).
3. Finally, keep track of the responses of your customers to each message. If a visitor clicks on a 'Special Offer', then make sure the other 'Special Offers' that are available remain visible on subsequent pages. If the customers clicks on the social proof email, then make sure the landing page features a number of 'bestselling' products.

By following these three simple steps, it is relatively easy to start implementing persuasion in your online communication and even to – limitedly – tailor it to the tastes of your customers. If you already use persuasion in your communication, then make sure you check whether or not you are stacking principles. And make sure that the customer experience is consistent: if the customer clicks on a product featuring one specific principle, then that principle should be featured on the next page too.

Principle	Possible implementations
Reciprocity	1. Allow your customers to try out your products for free
	2. Provide your customers with a free – no strings attached – information leaflet.
	3. Give 10 USD in virtual credits to your customers that they can directly cash in on your website.
Authority	1. Show the positive evaluations of experts next to your products.
	2. Follow Drew's example and create a list of Staff's recommended products.
	3. Use recommendations of famous authors if you are selling books, famous artists -music, or travel guides -holidays.
Social Proof	1. Show that specific products are bestsellers or otherwise popular.
	2. Show the evaluations of the product by different customers by means of 'likes', 'stars', etc.
	3. Show what other customers also bought or viewed after viewing a specific product.
Commitment	1. Create a wish-list that customers can use to add products that they might want to buy in the future.
	2. Make it easy for people to indicate that they like a product. Only offer the product for sale afterwards using the 'foot-in-the-door' technique.
	3. Make sure that your users can easily notify their friends or colleagues that they use your product. This will motivate them to buy the product again.

Liking	1. Use humor and wit in your content.
	2. Give visitors compliments about their browsing and searching behavior.
	3. Use real people (salespeople) who resemble your customers and allow them to chat in real time with your customers.
Scarcity	1. Emphasize scarcity in time: 'This product is only available for a week.'
	2. Emphasize scarcity in amount: 'There are only five pieces left.'
	3. Emphasize scarcity in availability: 'This product is only available for selected customers.'

Table 3: Examples of implementations of persuasion principles. Useful for adapting your online communication, or for recognizing when you – as a consumer – are being persuaded.

Obviously there are many other implementations of persuasion principles than those presented in Table 3 which can be created. You should really train yourself to recognize psychological influence attempts in communication: try to find at least two or three implementations of persuasion principles each time you visit an online store. If you can't find one, you probably need some more training. And, if you don't recognize persuasion it might be wise to activate your System II, instead of allowing continuous click-zoom responses from your System I.

I hope this brief section of practical tips – primarily added under pressure of my publisher – enables you to start working as an effective influencer. However, if you can actively use persuasion, then be aware that others can use it too. You will see more and more persuasive attempts in online content. And, increasingly these efforts will be personalized. Why? Well, because this increases the effect of online communication. However, the fact that it's effective does not necessarily imply that it's something we should strive for as a society. In the next Chapter, I will try to reflect upon the future of persuasion profiles. I will also discuss how they affect our autonomy and privacy.

Summarizing

In this chapter, I have described three examples of the successful use of persuasion profiles to increase impact. I have shown how persuasion profiles can motivate people to take the stairs, respond to an email, or buy more children's clothing. We have basically discussed the following:

- If you are able to identify individual customers,* present implementations of persuasion principles, and measure the effect of a message that is displayed to a customer you can start using persuasion profiles.
- Persuasion profiles can be created and used to motivate people to lead a healthier life, but they can also be used to sell more. In this chapter, persuasion profiles are regarded as a means to an end, irrespective of the end.
- The impact of persuasion profiles increases over time. As the number of interactions increases, the profile becomes more informed, and the impact increases.
- By using implementations of persuasion principles in your own communications and tracking their effect you can start persuading your customers.

---

* This one seems to be trickier and trickier due to legislation. We will see where it goes…

11

THE FUTURE OF PERSUASION PROFILES

Eleven-year-old Joey has resisted following his doctor's weight-loss plan – skipping his daily bike ride to play video games, trading his healthy lunches for soft drinks, and sneaking snacks at night. His dad Martin is frustrated. Concerned about some recent bullying, Martin goes online to check the parental control settings on his son's social network account. Martin sees something he's never noticed before – Joey's persuasion profile. Over his extensive use of the site, Joey has been shown countless ads for products, games, and other web sites. Each time, the site recorded Joey's response: Did he click on the ad? Did he play the game? Reading on, Martin learns that Joey rarely acts on recommendations from experts or celebrities but likes what his peers like and does what his peers do. Martin thinks, 'I wonder if we could use this to help Joey.' He finds an online weight loss program that helps kids motivate each other by sharing their successes.

This little scenario illustrates the possible future of persuasion profiles: they are created in one situation (on the social network) and are then used to persuade you in a different setting (the weight loss program). In the future, it might even be possible for outsiders, like Martin, to view your personal profile, to understand it and use it without your even knowing. Let's keep following Joey:

Joey can't sleep. He's too excited about going to school tomorrow wearing the new jeans his dad bought him. He's lost fifteen pounds over the last few months – earning many thumbs-up along the way from his

new friends online. He goes down to the kitchen to get a glass of water.
On the stairs, he overhears his parents talking – maybe about him.
'Such a miracle'... 'never would have done anything on his own'... 'good
thing I found out'... Found out what? Suddenly worried, Joey passes
the kitchen sink and quietly opens the fridge.

Persuasion profiles increase the impact of communication by personalizing the selection of persuasion principles. However, persuasion profiles are not by any means the only way in which we can create impact: we need to also target the right people and make the desired behavior as easy as possible to accomplish. So persuasion profiles are a next step in increasing impact. And, given the scientific evidence for the effects of persuasion profiles, they are potentially a strong driver of the impact of communication.

By now you know exactly what persuasion profiles are, and how they can be used to influence the behavior and attitudes of people. I believe that neither the online nor possible offline use of persuasion profiles can be stopped. It's only a matter of time before these profiles are used everywhere.* However, you are one of the first to know about them, so you will also be one of the first to think critically about their use.

In this final chapter of this book, I will try to answer several questions about the possible use of persuasion profiles. I will explain how they differ from other profiles that are already in use in online marketing. This allows you to better understand the potential threats and opportunities of persuasion profiles. I will try to discuss their ethical implications, and finally I will briefly reflect upon a possible world in which all the communication that we see is thoroughly personalized.

WHAT MAKES PERSUASION PROFILES DIFFERENT?

There are a number of ways in which persuasion profiles differ from other profiles or other forms of personalization that one can

---

* 'Persuasion' is currently hot amongst online marketers. Many consultancy agencies help companies on so-called 'persuasive design'. It is only a matter of time before these efforts are personalized.

encounter in marketing. Let us assume that persuasion profiles will become a current standard in online marketing. If so, then it's wise to think about the possible values and dangers of these profiles in advance. Persuasion profiles differ from traditional ways of personalization in at least two ways: persuasion profiles are end-independent, and they are likely to be less open than currently used profiles. Let's dig into both.

THE END-INDEPENDENCE OF PERSUASION PROFILES

Persuasion profiles are distinct from many others in marketing because they focus on the way a person can be influenced instead of focusing on the end goal of the attempt to influence. In Chapter 4 we discussed recommender systems: systems that select the right product for the right customer. The end-goal of the influence attempt is thus adjusted to your personal preference. This is a different focus from that of persuasion profiles: once the end-goal is clear, persuasion profiles can be used to determine how to best reach that goal.

This end-independence of persuasion profiles implies that profiles can be put to a much wider use than current profiles that are used for end personalization. If you, as an online bookseller, know that the current customer likes books about cycling then this information is of very limited value to your neighbor who sells domestic appliances. Or, when I know that you are looking for a new smartphone, that information is only valuable as long as you have not yet bought the phone: after you have made your choice, the information becomes meaningless. However, the fact that you respond better to the social proof principle than the authority principle, is information that is useful when I am selling you books, domestic appliances, and smartphones. Thus, your profile can be built up while you are browsing for books, and it can be used when offering you a new fridge. Your persuasion profile can be used independently of the end goal.

If you are not that similar to many others that I have talked to about this topic – using a social proof argument – then you are probably skeptical on this last point: you are inclined not to believe that you listen to the same type of arguments when you buy a book as when you buy a phone. Or, even more likely, the arguments that make you buy products will not be useful if I want to persuade you to take your medication on time. And that's a valid objection. The effects of distinct persuasion principles do indeed differ when we change the end goal. However, that fact does not threaten the end-independence of persuasion profiles: All that is required for end-independence is the fact that your response to a distinct principle compared to that of other people does not change when we move from one context to another.

End-independence is clearly illustrated in the story about Joey. Joey's father used the profile that was built up while Joey browsed his social network, and then applied the profile to a totally different situation; a new situation which was beneficial for his health. But remember, new situations might not always be desirable. Dean Eckles and I have described one of the worst-case scenarios in which the leaflet that you receive urging you to vote for a specific political party is personalized based on your online shopping behavior. The political party has bought your persuasion profile from an online store and is now using it to influence your voting behavior.*

Openness
End-independence persuasion profiles also differ from traditional profiles in their 'openness'. Or, rather, it is less likely for persuasion profiles to be disclosed to consumers than for other marketing profiles. For recommendation systems and the profiles they maintain, there is quite a lot of evidence that disclosure of the profile increases impact.** It is apparently quite a good idea to tell consumers that products have been especially selected for them based on their preferences. So the use of recommender systems is often made explicit. It is clear to consumers that their preferences

---

* This worst-case scenario almost came true right after a story on Persuasion Profiles was published in Wired: Dean Eckles and I were approached by a political party. We refused.
** A number of studies point in this direction. See: Gretzel & Fesenmaier, 2006 or Sukumaran, Vezich, McHugh & Nass, 2011.

are being tracked, and that these preferences are being used to recommend products.

However, it is very likely that disclosure of the profile is not at all a good thing for persuasion profiles. Steven Duplisnky (who we met in Chapter 7) and I once carried out a small study into this: we looked at the effect of different persuasion profiles when the use of that profile was either disclosed or not disclosed to the recipient. The results of the study were very clear and in line with other efforts in this direction: if you tell people that you are actively persuading them using persuasion principles, then the attempt to influence is likely to fail. A logical explanation for this is that people become wary once you tell them that you are using persuasion, and their processing moves from System I to System II. As more and more elaborate processing takes place, influence attempts using persuasion principles will become less effective. Thus, unlike end-personalization, the personalization of the means of an influence attempt is likely not to be disclosed to consumers since disclosure is likely to defeat the purpose of the attempt to influence. For influencers it is beneficial not to disclose the fact that they are trying to persuade.

However, the study that I conducted with Steven also revealed something else: if you let people choose their own persuasion principle then this can and does increase the impact. In our study, we had a group of people choose whether they preferred expert advice, or advice from a group of their friends. If the influence attempt that we tried after this corresponded to their choice, it was more successful. So, if you tell people that you are influencing them, it negatively effects compliance. On the other hand, if they can choose themselves which arguments are used against them this positively affects compliance.

Based on these results, I think it will be possible to disclose the use of persuasion profiles without fully defeating their purpose. And I also think that disclosure is socially desirable. However, we still need to develop ways in which the use of persuasion profiles can be disclosed without reducing their effect.

In the end, openness should not just be a choice made by influencers based on the effects of their attempts to influence. Open-

ness and disclosure of the use of persuasion profiles are likely to be
regulated in the future. In the Netherlands and most of Europe,
fairly strict rules already exist for the use of cookies online: hence
the methods of tracking individuals are already severely regulated.
These regulations are likely to become even stricter, and they will
restrict the freedom of influencers to build profiles and change
messages. Of course I am not completely sure of this, but I believe
that within five years, the practice of creating a persuasion profile
in one context (e.g. a bookstore) and using it in another context
(e.g. for a political party) is likely to be banned. Now, whether
these regulations will indeed force people to be 'open' in their use
of persuasion profiles or not, only time will tell.*

COMBINING PERSUASION PROFILES WITH EXISTING PROFILES

In this book I have discussed the use of persuasion profiles to increase the impact – and thus the final effect – of online attempts
to influence. This new step in personalization is the logical next
step in the quest of influencers to increase their impact. It is likely
that persuasion profiles will not be used in isolation in the future,
but in conjunction with other types of personalization. Persuasion profiles will likely be combined with behavioral targeting and
recommender systems to make sure that you are pitched the right
product in the right way.**

Persuasion profiles are likely also to be combined with other
types of online marketing. It is likely that persuasion profiles will
be more deeply integrated into the current profiling practice. We
have already seen that meta-judgments (answers to questionnaires)
can be used to estimate the effect of persuasion principles. And it is
likely that relationships between the effect of persuasion principles
and age and gender also exist. Thus, it is likely that this type of
information will be used to make sure that your persuasion profile
is even more accurate than it would be if it were derived from your

---

* Currently there is quite a big gap between the legislation in Europe and
that in the US. However, it seems that the recent NSA revelations are spar-
king a world-wide discussion on the topic.
** And yes, at the *right* time. The trick is to determine what is right.

behavior alone. Likely demographics, location, and many other types of information will at least be used to kick-start your profile when you newly arrive at an online store.

In the long run, I believe most of the profiling that is done in marketing will be based solely on behavior: at least if this practice is not severely regulated. We now have the opportunity to track customers for an indefinite time, over a number of stores. While demographics, age, and location were invaluable pieces of information in tailoring communication twenty years ago, their value is diminishing due to our ability to directly measure customer behavior. It is likely that old forms of segmentation based only on age, gender, and the like will disappear in the future.

ARE PERSUASION PROFILES ETHICALLY 'ALLOWED'?

Persuasion profiles will change the future of online marketing. It is my hope that by now you have good insight into what the possible impact these profiles can have. What remains is the question of whether or not we actually want persuasion profiles. If you are a naïve influencer and just trying to sell more – and you do not think about the consequences – then the answer is simple: Yes! But if you are a consumer yourself (which you are) or if you contemplate the consequences of using persuasion profiles, then the answer might not be so straightforward. Now, I have to say that I myself am not an ethicist, and I cannot decide for you whether you should promote or reject persuasion profiles. But I will try to give my opinion regarding the most pressing ethical considerations of the use of persuasion profiles.

In some ways, those who influence others are always in an uneasy ethical position. There are quite few researchers who work on persuasive technology who agree that the ethical consequences of these types of technology are unclear. However, a number of researchers have attempted to assist those building persuasive technologies in making the 'correct' ethical choices. Two prominent scholars in this field are Berdichevsky and Neuenschwander.[*] As far back as 1999, before persuasive technologies were common-

---

[*] See for the original article: Berdichevsky & Neuenschwander, 1999.

place, they were discussing their ethical implications. Their basic premise is the following: if the end-goal of a persuasive technology is ethically sound, then the creator of the technology is on the right track.

Based on this simple idea those who use persuasion profiles to help other lose weight are heroes, while those who use the exact same persuasion profiles to sell cigarettes are villains.*

Nowadays many scholars in the persuasive technology field create technologies that have very noble aims. They create technologies that help people stay active, or help people make wise decisions (according to the designer of the technology). Or they make technologies that help users reduce their energy consumption. These types of applications, according to Berdichevsky and Neuenschwander, are ethically feasible, and thus designers of these applications are doing the right thing. If we used persuasion profiles to increase the impact of these technologies, then this would be ethically sound.

Personally however I find this too narrow an ethical assessment of persuasion profiles. An assessment based on the end-goal is too limited if the same profile can also be used or misused for other goals. The end-goal itself should not be the only decisive element in determining whether or not we should use persuasion profiles. In my opinion we need another method of evaluating them than that suggested by Berdichevsky and Neuenschwander.

Haworth, a contemporary philosopher, has provided a structured framework for thinking about the impact of new technologies and the associated ethical implications.** Haworth describes two concepts that are often the underlying cause of ethical dilemmas caused by new technologies: the technology threatens either the privacy or the autonomy of its users; or both. Let's examine the ethics of persuasion profiling using these two criteria.

---

*   In this definition a way to determine a 'good' end-goal is obviously needed. However, this question is not answered by the authors.
**   Haworth, inspired by Dworkins, writes about the impact of technology on privacy and autonomy. See: Haworth, 1991.

Privacy

Privacy originates from the Latin word 'privatus', which means 'to keep for oneself' in the sense of 'not disclosing' as opposed to 'remembering'. Privacy, in the scientific literature on the topic, is often referred to as the ability of individuals to conceal from the outside world some piece of personal information. People deem objects or thoughts private when they are unwilling to share these openly. A lot of new technologies threaten our privacy.

Persuasion profiles threaten our privacy because the information in them might be regarded as private. We may not want to share with our partner or neighbor or the rest of the world which persuasion principles affect us. However, persuasion profiles are certainly not the only carriers of sensitive information that can be found online. Other digital profiles have been the topic of discussions on privacy, and I do not think that persuasion profiles really offer a novel threat. Just as you might not like your personal information – such as the knowledge that you are reading this book while sitting on the toilet – to be shared, you probably do not want your persuasion profile to be shared. You digital privacy has rightfully led to heated debate. There are numerous examples of houses that are broken into because the inhabitants unknowingly alerted a burglar via Twitter of the fact that they were on holiday. Some information should probably be kept private. Despite the possible negative effects of disclosing too much information, some people do share with the world that they are currently on the toilet...

Researchers in the field of ubiquitous computing – a field that studies systems in which computation power is everywhere around us – have structurally discussed the impact of new technologies on privacy. They often relate to the proportionality principle in discussions on privacy: if you disclose information, make it non-private, then this can be deemed ethical only if you receive something in return. And, really, whatever you get in return should outweigh the costs of giving up your privacy. So, if you tell me that you like books on cycling, then the disclosure of this information is ethical if I actually end up giving you a better book recommendation.

The principle of proportionality however is fairly hard to use when evaluating persuasion profiles. If you disclose your profile when using an activity monitor (or similar technology) to help you lose weight, you might believe that the benefits are plenty and thus that the breach of privacy is ethical. This in no way means that you want this exact same information to be passed on to a political party. So while you are willing to disclose some information for a specific purpose, you do not intend that this same act might lead to your privacy being violated for another. I currently really do not believe that there is a clear answer to the privacy questions that are raised by persuasion profiling.

For now however, I do think it's safe to conclude that persuasion profiles do not pose a novel threat to privacy. They should be evaluated in conjunction with other profiles, including your Facebook and Twitter profiles. I believe that, in part, the current threats should already be regulated: if we look at the current online behavior of people, it seems that we have a hard time foreseeing the possible negative effects of disclosing a lot of personal information.

Autonomy

In addition to the privacy hazard, persuasion profiles might also jeopardize our autonomy; Haworth's second criterion. Autonomy concerns the ability of individuals to make their own decisions. The question becomes whether choices that are made using a persuasion profile are still choices that you would make based on your own free will or if you are being 'forced' by external powers.*

Many of the studies about persuasion – which form the basis of persuasion profiles – show that people are often unaware of the effect of persuasion. People use System I, and are unconsciously persuaded.** Even more so, if we alert people to the use of persuasion principles, their power of persuasion often diminishes. Thus, it would seem that persuasion profiles are a direct and severe attack on our autonomy: persuasion profiles influence our decision up

---

* Whether we have a true 'free will' is not something philosophers agree on. So I will not dwell on this point too long.
** Quite a lot of studies on this topic can be found. However, I would recommend: Cacioppo, Petty, Kao & Rodriguez, 1986.

to the point where we take actions that we would not have taken otherwise. Thus, our behavior, under the influence of persuasion profiles, is not directed by our free will but by outside forces.

This might be the main source of unease that people feel when first reading about persuasion profiles. Nevertheless, I believe the threat that persuasion profiles pose to our autonomy can also be an opportunity. When a persuasion profile is created based on your behavior – and not based on some questionnaire – then the profile might contain information that you yourself are not even aware of. You might believe that you buy products because of their amazing price-quality trade-off, but in reality you are just buying whatever is popular. If you could understand your own profile from this perspective, this might allow you to learn something new about yourself. Therefore, you could inspect your persuasion profile and use it to make more informed decisions in the future. Thus, persuasion profiles could actually be used as a learning tool to increase our autonomy in the long run.

I do not think persuasion profiles pose a direct threat to our autonomy. However, to be an opportunity rather than a threat, persuasion profiles should be disclosed.

THE FUTURE: YOUR OWN BUBBLE

Predictions are difficult to make! However, I am quite sure that persuasion profiles – and other forms of personalized marketing – will be the future of online marketing. The practical problems that hindered online conversion rates have been solved, and we have the ability to reach out to anyone we want to reach. The final effect of online communication will depend on the impact of the communication and I do not believe that the difference between a light or dark blue background, or a button with rounded or square corners, is going to give a competitive edge. Future impact will be achieved by considering the ways in which people make decisions. More and more influencers will use psychological principles, and our tendency to use System I, to increase their impact.

Persuasion profiles are only a part of this future. There are important psychological traits that can be derived from your browsing behavior. A fairly recent study by Dean Eckles and Mike

Nowak, for example, showed that we can predict the personality of people based on their comments on a social networking site. Dean and Mike took thousands of users of a social network and measured their personality using a questionnaire. Afterwards, they tried to see if they could predict the observed personality scores using an analysis of the texts that people wrote on the social network. The researchers thus tried to determine their personalities automatically, by having a computer analyze the comments of users, This went surprisingly well: solely based on the textual comments, it is possible to create a crude personality profile.* Obviously, this personality profile can then be used to personalize advertisements. Persuasion profiles are only one of the many ways by which the Internet can be personalized.

What the Internet will present to you will be determined by your personal purchasing and click behavior. However, this behavior might not correspond exactly to your actual preferences. The divergence of actual preferences and the criteria that are used for personalization is already visible online. Authors like Eli Pariser argue that the personalization of the Internet will have a profound effect on our daily lives.**

The argument is as follows: suppose you read an online news story about a political party: say you are reading about the Democrats. The news you are reading is slightly negative in tone, and the leader of the party is criticized. Technically it is already possible to discern this negative feeling in the text without any human intervention. You end up clicking a link in the article. More specifically, you click a restaurant ad that is displayed next to the article. Your click on the restaurant ad trains the system in such a way that it learns that you are likely to click on ads after seeing negative articles about the Democrats. While many positive articles about the Democrats are likely to be available, these will not be shown to

---

* The researchers used the so-called Big Five personality scale, see: Gosling, Rentfrow & Swann, 2003. The study itself can be found in: Eckles, Nowak & Wieland, 2012.
** See, Pariser, 2011.

you in the future: you see negative articles since these articles seem to be the ones that make you click on ads. Because the system tries to optimize your clicks, you end up reading – possibly for months on end – solely negative articles. In your own, personalized, online world the Democrats are a weird bunch about whom no good article has ever been written.

The articles that I am shown might look very different. I chose, quite coincidentally, a positive message the first time I got to the news site. And while you forwarded the negative message to me, I never read it. So, the personalization system figured out that I like positive messages about the Democrats. For me, after a few months, the Democrats are a thriving party with a great program and an amazing leader.

You and I thus both live in our own isolated worlds. We live in our own bubbles. Our bubbles however are not created based on our interest, but are rather based on our click behavior. The articles we see are deprived of any nuance. And our worlds might be growing apart. Perhaps they diverge up to the point at which, if we ever meet in the physical world, our opinions and arguments would differ so much that we would end up quarreling.

This really is the doomsday scenario of extensive personalization. It contains some strong ideas: it is already virtually impossible to objectively evaluate the value of the information that is served to us. Additionally, it is indeed true that providing complete and balanced information is not at all the aim of current personalization algorithms. The personalized information is not necessarily the information we want to see.

We should remember that when the radio was invented many researchers wrote lengthy doomsday stories about it. The same thing happened when television arrived. However, none of these scares ever came true. So it remains to be seen whether the personal Internet bubble created by our personalization algorithms will eventually be a real problem.

CONCLUSION

I could end this book with a bulleted list summarizing most of it, as I did for the previous chapters. However, I will not. I promised in the introduction that I would explain how persuasion profiles can be used to increase the impact of online marketing, and to that end I hope I have been successful.

In any case, by now you know why the effect of online communication has not been what it could have been: with the increase of its reach the impact apparently dropped. This is the primary reason why the effect of digital technologies is not nearly as wide as expected solely based on its tremendous range.

Additionally, I hope by now you also have a clear idea why our first attempts to increase impact failed: we targeted the wrong people and presented them with too many choices. Because of this we now spend serious efforts reaching the right people and narrowing down, automatically, the choices that consumers were confronted with. And, we made sure that websites were 'user friendly' so that everyone was able to buy products and services.

But still the impact was lagging behind. It was better than in the early days, but still not where it could be. This was partly due to the fact that we forgot to focus on those things that actually drive human decisions: we forgot about peripheral processing. Basically, we refrained from using the 'weapons of influence' that had proven so tremendously effective in face-to-face communication. And, even when we did consider these weapons, we forgot that people are different and their reactions differ. Even if you know exactly which product someone is looking for, you still need to know how to communicate. Which message do you actually use to persuade people?

Persuasion profiles describe for each persuasion strategy how individuals will respond to them. So they describe which persuasion strategies people are susceptible to. With an accurate persuasion profile at hand – created based on your online behavior – we can improve the impact of computer-human communication. Online marketers can select, automatically, those principles that you are susceptible to, increasing the chance that you will be persuaded. The effects of persuasion are likely much stronger than those of the background color of a webpage or the shape of a button, and thus it is very likely that persuasion profiles will be heavily used by influencers in days to come. Every time you respond, your profile will become more precise.

But, persuasion profiles cannot just be used against you. Persuasion profiles can help you learn more about your own decisions. If you know your profile, you can guard yourself against unwanted influence attempts. For example, you can consciously start searching for the use of those persuasion strategies that you are susceptible to. You can force yourself to use System II, and make decisions based on elaborate reasoning. You will display fewer click-zoom responses, and this might change your future decisions.*

It is ultimately up to you whether you fancy a world in which persuasion profiles are omnipresent. However, I think it's fair warning to state that persuasion profiles are only a symptom of a new unfolding world. This will be a world in which you cannot just consume all the information you like, but all the information that you consume will reveal something about you. This might make your life much easier – if you search for a restaurant it will be convenient if the ones that surface are in your neighborhood. However, things might not turn out completely positive: there are already countries in which a 'wrong' online friend can get you into solitary confinement or worse. What will prevail... only time will tell.

---

* It 'might': if the same argument is also effective via System II, we will end up making the same decision.

EPILOGUE

If I assume for convenience that you are reading this book from front to back, then by now you will have read most of it. All that is left is this short epilogue.

I hope this book has helped you to understand how to create impact in online communication. I have tried to summarize some of the major studies in social psychology that explain why certain attempts to influence are successful, but I have also presented some of my own work on persuasion profiling. Hidden in between these sections I have tried to give a bit of insight into the technologies that currently make the web simple and effective. I truly hope that you have learned something new.

Before finishing though, I would like to put some of the developments that I describe into perspective. I think persuasion profiles as I describe in this book are impending. And, I believe many other techniques that rely on deriving your preferences, interests, and weaknesses from you behavior will steadily emerge in online marketing. This happens to be the reality that we live in. This is a reality in which each interaction that we have with technology not only teaches us something, but also discloses something personal and possibly private. Whatever we disclose will be used by others to influence our behavior, to sell us products, or to get us to vote for a specific political party.

Persuasion profiles are a first step on the road to the increased impact of online communication. The persuasion principles that we have discussed originate from the systematic study of human-to-human influence and have proven to be effective. This however does not mean that these principles cover all we need to know: it's likely that many other principles exist and that we can learn more about, and become better at, persuading others using online communication.

In the future everything you do will be stored in a profile. And every sales pitch directed at you will disclose meaningful information about you. This increases the impact, and eventually the effect, of online communication.

From the large number of talks I have given over the last year on the topic of persuasion profiling, I have noticed that many people believe all of this might happen in some distant future. This is not at all true: persuasion profiles are happening right now. They are everywhere, and their use will only grow. Many people still believe that they are relatively anonymous online: this is not true at all. We must learn to accept that online communication is two-way. If you look up a phone number on a phone number website, you might think that this interaction resembles looking up a phone number in a book – which is what we used to do a bit over a decade ago. However, this is not true: if you look up a phone number online someone will know that you looked it up. Where you were when you looked it up. What time it was. And which other numbers you looked up previously. If you are calling a real-estate broker in a village close to the city where you live for the third time you might be looking for property. And, since the brokers that you call are those that are well evaluated by others, you seem to be susceptible to social proof. This knowledge can and will be used to sell you property. None of this would have happened in the early days – when you looked up phone numbers in a book – but currently it is our reality. And whether we decide to like it or not, I think we should first be aware of it. I hope this book has helped to create a bit of that awareness.

Writing a book is not something one does by oneself. I obviously had a lot of help. This book is translated from the Dutch, partly by myself. However, I have been fortunate enough to receive a lot of help from Michael Klazema and Ronald Voorn on the initial translation. Afterwards my editor, in a joint effort with Cheryl McClain took quite some time to take my mixture of Dutch and English and turn it into the book you have just read. I would like to thank them for all their help. Besides those who helped on the translation, many others helped to get the initial Dutch version together. Most notably:

- My publisher, Business Contact, and especially my editor Sandra Wouters. Without her you would have been reading a fairly bad book by now. If this book is a pleasant read in any way, that's her accomplishment.
- My colleagues with whom I have done research in recent years –most of whom I've explicitly mentioned in the text. I would like to call particular attention to Dean Eckles, Professor Panos Markopoulos, Dr. Boris de Ruyter, Professor Clifford Nass and Prof. Emile Aarts.
- My colleagues at Science Rock Stars & PersuasionAPI. With a special mention for Arjan Haring who got things to start (and keep) rolling.
- My friends.
- My parents and my brother (and his wife and two – almost three – great kids!).
- Rosa (she's cool).

Thank you for reading!

REFERENCES

In case you want to know more about the topics that I tough upon in this book, please have a look at the original articles. They are referred to in the footnotes. Here you find the full reference.

Allen, R. B. (1997). Mental Models and User Models. In M. Helander, T. K. Landauer, & P. Prabhu (Eds.), *Handbook of Human Computer Interaction* (Vol. 1, pp. 49-63). Elsevier Science B.V.

Amabile, T. M., & Glazebrook, A. H. A. (1982). A negativity bias in interpersonal evaluation. *Journal of Experimental Social Psychology*, 18, 1-22.

Aral, S., Muchnik, L., & Sundararajan, A. (2009). Distinguishing influence-based contagion from homophily-driven diffusion in dynamic networks. *Proceedings of the National Academy of Sciences of the United States of America*, 106(51), 21544-21549.

Aral, S., Muchnik, L., & Sundararajan, A. (2011). Engineering Social Contagions : Optimal Network Seeding and Incentive Strategies. *Available at SSRN: http://ssrn.com/abstract=1770982*.

Ariely, D. (2008). *Predictably Irrational: The Hidden Forces That Shape Our Decisions*. HarperCollins.

Asch, S. E. (1955). Opinions and Social Pressure. (A. P. Hare, E. F. Borgatta, & R. F. Bales, Eds.) *Scientific American*, 193(5), 31-35.

Asch, S. E. (1956). Studies of independence and conformity: A minority of one against a unanimous majority. *Psychological Monographs*, 70(9), 1-70.

Baker, S. (2009). Learning, and Profiting, from Online Friendships. *Business-Week*, 9(22).

Baran. (2005). *Introduction to Mass Communication*. McGraw-Hill Publishing Co.

Barry, B., & Shapiro, D. L. (1992). Influence Tactics in Combination: The Interactive Effects of Soft Versus Hard Tactics and Rational Exchange. *Journal of Applied Social Psychology*, 22(18), 1429-1441.

Bassili, J. N. (1996). Meta-judgmental versus operative indexes of psychological attributes: The case of measures of attitude strength. *Journal of Personality and Social Psychology*, 71(4), 637-653.

Baumeister, R. F., & Leary, M. R. (1995). The need to belong: desire for interpersonal attachments as a fundamental human motivation. *Psychological Bulletin*, 117(3), 497-529.

Berdichevsky, D., & Neuenschwander, E. (1999). Toward an ethics of persuasive technology. *Communications of the ACM*, 42(5), 51-58.

Berger, C. R. (1975). Task performance and attributional communication as determinants of interpersonal attraction. *Speech Monographs*, 40, 280–286.

Bless, H., Bohner, G., Schwarz, N., & Strack, F. (1990). Mood and Persuasion. *Personality and Social Psychology Bulletin*, 16(2), 331-345.

Booth-Butterfield, S., & Welbourne, J. (2002). The Elaboration Likelihood Model: Its Impact on Persuasion Theory and Research. In J. P. Dillard & M. W. Pfau (Eds.), *The Persuasion Handbook Developments in Theory and Practice* (pp. 195-211). Sage.

Burger, J. M. (1999). The Foot-in-the-Door Compliance Procedure: A Multiple-Process Analysis and Review. *Personality and Social Psychology Review*, 3(4), 303-325.

Cacioppo, J T, & Petty, R. E. (1982). The need for Cognition. *Journal of Personality and Social Psychology.*, 42(1), 116-131.

Cacioppo, J T, Petty, R. E., Kao, C. F., & Rodriguez, R. (1986). Central and peripheral routes to persuasion: An individual difference perspective. *Journal of Personality and Social Psychology*, 51(5), 1032–1043.

Cacioppo, John T, Petty, R. E., & Kao, C. F. (1984). The Efficient Assessment of Need for Cognition. *Journal of Personality Assessment*, 48(3), 306.

Cialdini, R B, Trost, M. R., & Newsom, J. T. (1995). Preference for consistency: The development of a valid measure and the discovery of surprising behavioral implications. *Journal of Personality and Social Psychology*, 69, 318-328.

Cialdini, R. (2001). *Influence, Science and Practice*. Boston: Allyn & Bacon.

Cialdini, R B, & Trost, M. R. (1998). Social Influence: Social Norms, Conformity, and Compliance. In D. T. Gilbert, S. T. Fiske, & G. Lindzey (Eds.), *The Handbook of Social Psychology* (Vol. 2, pp. 151-192). McGraw-Hill.

Cialdini, Robert B. (2005). Don't Throw in the Towel: Use Social Influence Research. *American Psychological Society Observer*, 18(4), 33-34.

Danzico, L. (2010). The Design of Serendipity Is Not by Chance. *Interactions*, 17, 16-18.

Davis, B. P., & Knowles, E. S. (1999). A disrupt-then-reframe technique of social influence. *Journal of Personality and Social Psychology*, 76, 192-199.

Eckles, D., Nowak, M., & Wieland, J. (2012). Manifestations of Personality in Online Communicaiton. *Working Paper*.

Eisend, M. (2008). Explaining The Impact Of Scarcity Appeals In Advertising: The Mediating Role of Perceptions of Susceptibility. *Journal of Advertising*, 37(3), 33-40.

Fogg, B. J., & Nass, C. (1997). Silicon sycophants: the effects of computers that flatter. *International Journal of Human-Computer Studies*, 46(5), 551-561.

Falbe, C. M., & Yukl, G. (2008). Consequences for Managers of Using Single Influence Tactics and Combinations of Tactics. *The Academy of Management Journal*.

Festinger, L. (1957). *A Theory of Cognitive Dissonance*. Stanford University Press.

Fiske, S. T. (1980). Attention and weight in person perception: The impact of negative and extreme behavior. *Journal of Personality and Social Psychology*, 36, 889-906.

Fogg, B. J. (2002). *Persuasive Technology: Using Computers to Change What We Think and Do*. Morgan Kaufmann.

Fogg, B. J. (2009). The Behavior Grid: 35 ways behavior can change. In S. Chatterjee & P. Dev (Eds.), *Persuasive Technology, Fourth International Conference, PERSUASIVE 2009*, Claremont, California, {USA}, April 26-29, 2009..

Fogg, B. J., & Eckles, D. (2007). *Mobile Persuasion: 20 Perspectives on the Future of Behavior Change*. In B. J. Fogg & D. Eckles (Eds.), Mobile Persuasion (pp. 1-166). Stanford Captology Media.

Freedman, J. L., & Fraser, S. C. (1966). Compliance without pressure: The foot-in-the-door technique. *Journal of Personality and Social Psychology*, 4, 195-202.

Garner, R. (2005). What's in a Name? Persuasion Perhaps. *Journal of Consumer Psychology*, 15, 108-116.

Golan, G. J., & Zaidner, L. (2008). Creative Strategies in Viral Advertising: An Application of Taylor's Six-Segment Message Strategy Wheel. *Journal of*

Computer-Mediated Communication, 13(4), 959-972.

Goldstein, N. J., Cialdini, R. B., & Griskevicius, V. (2008). A Room with a Viewpoint: Using Social Norms to Motivate Environmental Conservation in Hotels. *Journal of Consumer Research*, 35(3), 472-482.

Gosling, S. D., Rentfrow, P. J., & Swann W. B., J. (2003). A very brief measure of the Big-Five personality domains. *Journal of Research in Personality*, 37, 504-528.

Gretzel, U., & Fesenmaier, D. (2006). Persuasion in Recommender Systems. *International Journal of Electronic Commerce*, 11(2), 81-100.

Guadagno, R., & Cialdini, R. (2005). Online persuasion and compliance: Social influence on the Internet and beyond. In Y. Amichai-Hamburger (Ed.), *The Social Net: Understanding human behavior in cyberspace* (p. 296).

Haugtvedt, C. P., Petty, R. E., & Cacioppo, J. T. (1992). Need for Cognition and Advertising: Understanding the Role of Personality Variables in Consumer Behavior. *Journal of Consumer Psychology*, 1(3), 239-260.

Hauser, J. R., Urban, G. L., Liberali, G., & Braun, M. (2009). Website Morphing. *Marketing Science*, 28(2), 202-223.

Haworth, L. L. (1991). Dworkin on Autonomy. *Ethics*, 102(1).

Hollis. (2007). *Rational Economic Man*. Cambridge University Press.

Hornstain, H. A., Fisch, E., & Holmes, M. (1968). Influence of a model's feeling about his behavior and his relevance as a comparison other on obervers' helping behavior. *Journal of Personality and Social Psychology*, 10, 222-226.

Hutchinson, J. W., Kamakura, W. A., & Lynch, J. J. G. (2001). Unobserved Heterogeneity as an Alternative Explanation for ``Reversal" Effects in Behavioral Research. *Journal of Consumer Research*, 27(3), 324-344.

Jarvis, W. B. G., & Petty, R. E. (1996). The need to evaluate. *Journal of Personality and Social Psychology*, 70(1), 172-194.

Johnson, D., Gardner, J., & Wiles, J. (2004). Experience as a moderator of the media equation: the impact of flattery and praise. *International Journal of Human-Computer Studies*, 61(3), 237-258.

Kahneman, D. (2011). *Thinking, Fast and Slow*. Farrar, Straus and Giroux.

Kaptein, M. C., de Ruyter, B., Markopoulos, P., & Aarts, E. H. L. (2009). *Simple Ways to Make Friends*. In the Proceedings of the 8th International Workshop on Social Intelligence.

Kaptein, M. (2012). Personalized Persuasion in Ambient Intelligence. *Doctoral Thesis from the Eindhoven University of Technology*.

Kaptein, M. C. (2011). Adaptive Persuasive Messages in an E-commerce Setting: The use of Persuasion Profiles. *Proceedings of ECIS 2011*. Helsinki.

Kaptein, M.C., & Duplinsky, S. (2012). Combining Multiple Influence Strategies to Increase Consumer Compliance. *International Journal of Internet Marketing and Advertising*, in press.

Kaptein, M. C., Duplinsky, S., & Markopoulos, P. (2011). Means based adaptive persuasive systems. *Proceedings of the 2011 annual conference on Human factors in computing systems* (pp. 335-344). New York, NY, USA: ACM.

Kaptein, M. C., & Eckles, D. (2012). Heterogeneity in the Effects of Online Persuasion. *Journal of Interactive Marketing*, Available at: http://dx.doi.org/10.1016/j.intmar.2012.02.002

Kaptein, M. C., Eckles, D., & Davis, J. (2011). Envisioning Persuasion Profiles: Challenges for Public Policy and Ethical Practice. ACM *Interactions*, 18(5), 66-69.

Kaptein, M. C., & Robertson, J. (2012). Rethinking Statistical Methods for HCI. *Proceedings of the 2011 annual conference on Human factors in computing systems*, CHI 212. 1105-1114.

Kaptein, M. C., de Ruyter, B., Markopoulos, P., & Aarts, E. (2011). Tailored Persuasive Text Messages to Reduce Snacking. *Transactions on Interactive Intelligent Systems*, 2(2), 1-25.

Kaptein, M. C., & van Halteren, A. (2012). Adaptive Persuasive Messaging to Increase Service Retention. *Journal of Personal and Ubiquitous Computing*, Available at: http://dx.doi.org/10.1007/s00779-012-0585-3

Kardes, F. R., Fennis, B. M., Hirt, E. R., Tormala, Z. L., & Bullington, B. (2007). The role of the need for cognitive closure in the effectiveness of the disrupt-then-reframe influence technique. *Journal of Consumer Research*, 34(3), 377-385.

Komorita, S. S., Hilty, J. A., & Parks, C. D. (1991). Reciprocity and Cooperation in Social Dilemmas. (U. Schulz, W. Albers, & U. Mueller, Eds.) *Journal of Conflict Resolution*, 35(3), 494-518. Springer-Verlag.

Kostakos, V. (2008). Using Bluetooth to capture passenger trips on public transport buses. *CoRR*. Available at: http://arxiv.org/abs/0806.0874

Lindholm, J., Parvinen, P., & Kaptein, M. C. (2012). The Dangers of Engagement: How Substitution in Online Services Leads to Decreasing Revenues. under submission.

Lynn, M. (1991). Scarcity effects on value: A quantitative review of the commodity theory literature. *Psychology and Marketing*, 8(1), 43-57.

Mackie, D. M. (1986). Social identification effects in group polarization. *Journal of Personality and Social Psychology*, 50(4), 720-728.

Manski, C.F. (2008). Actualist rationality. *Theory and Decision*, 1–16.

Milgram, S. (1974). Obedience to Authority. London: Tavistock.

Myers, D. G., & Lamm, H. (1976). The group polarization phenomenon. *Psychological Bulletin*, 83, 602-627.

Nail, P. R., Correll, J. S., Drake, C. E., Glenn, S. B., Scott, G. M., & Stuckey, C. (2001). A validation study of the preference for consistency scale. *Personality and Individual Differences*, 31, 1193-1202.

Nass, C., Fogg, B. J., & Moon, Y. (1996). Can computers be teammates? *International Journal of Human-Computer Studies*, 45(6), 669-678.

Nass, C., Steuer, J., Henriksen, L., & Dryer, D. C. (1994). Machines, social attributions, and ethopoeia: performance assessments of computers subsequent to 'self-' or 'other-' evaluations. *International Journal of Human-Computer Studies*, 40(3), 543-559.

Nissani, M. (1990). A cognitive reinterpretation of Stanley Milgram's observations on obedience to authority. *Amarican Psychologist*, 45, 1384-1385.

Ochi, P., Rao, S., Takayama, L., & Nass, C. (2010). Predictors of user perceptions of web recommender systems: How the basis for generating experience and search product recommendations affects user responses. *International Journal of Human-Computer Studies*, 68(8), 472-482.

Opper, M. (1997). A Bayesian Approach to Online Learning. In Saad, David (ed.). *On-line learning in neural networks*. Publications of the Newton Institute.

Packer, D. J. (2008). Identifying Systematic Disobedience in Milgram's Obedience Experiments: A Meta-Analytic Review. *Perspectives on Psychological Science*, 3(4), 301-304. SAGE Publications.

Page, L., Brin, S., Rajeev, M., & Winograd, T. (1999). *The PageRank Citation Ranking: Bringing Order to the Web*. Technical Report. Stanford Infolab. http://ilpubs.stanford.edu:8090/422/

Pallak, M. S., Cook, D. A., & Sullivan, J. J. (1980). Commitment and energy conservation. (L. Bickman, Ed.) *Applied Social Psychology Annual*, 1, Medium: X; Size: Pages: 235-253. Sage.

Pariser, E. (2011). *The Filter Bubble*. Penguin Press.

Petty, E. P., & Cacioppo, J. T. (1986). The Elaboration Likelihood Model of Persuasion. *Advances in Experimental Social Psychology*, 19.

Petty, R. E., & Wegener, D. T. (1999). The elaboration likelihood model: Current status and controversies. In S. Chaiken & Y. Trope (Eds.), *Dual-process theories in social psychology* (p. 41-72). New York: Guilford Press.

Reeves, B., & Nass, C. (1996). *The Media Equation: How People Treat Computers, Television, and New Media Like Real People and Places.* Cambridge University Press.

Ricci, F., Rokach, L., Shapira, B., & Kantor, P. B. (2011). *Recommender Systems Handbook.* (F. Ricci, L. Rokach, B. Shapira, & P. B. Kantor, Eds.) Media, 54(11), 217-253. Springer US.

Rogers, E. M. (1995). *Diffusion of Innovations.* Simon and Schuster.

Rosen, S., & Tesser, A. (1970). On reluctance to communicate undesirable information: The MUM effect. *Sociometry, 33,* 588-599.

Sakai, R., Peteghem, S. van, Sande, L. van de, Banach, P., & Kaptein, M. C. (2011). Personalized Persuasion in Ambient Intelligence: the APStairs System. *Proceedings of Ambient Intelligence (AmI) 2011.* Amsterdam.

Schwartz, B. (2003). *The Paradox of Choice: Why More Is Less.* Ecco.

Scott, S. L. (2010). A modern Bayesian look at the multi-armed bandit. *Applied Stochastic Models in Business and Industry, 26*(6), 639-658.

Stein, C. (1955). Inadmissibility of the Usual Estimator for the Mean of a Multivariate Normal Distribution. *Proceedings of the Third Berkeley Symposium on Mathematical Statistics and Probability,* 197-206.

Sukumaran, A., Vezich, S., McHugh, M., & Nass, C. (2011). Normative influences on thoughtful online participation. *Proceedings of the 2011 annual conference on Human factors in computing systems – CHI '11* (p. 3401). New York, New York, USA: ACM Press.

Tajfel, H. (1982). Social identity and intergroup relations. *Contemporary Sociology* (Vol. 14, p. 520). Cambridge University Press.

Verhallen, T. M. M., & Robben, H. S. J. (1994). Scarcity and preference: An experiment on unavailability and product evaluation. *Journal of Economic Psychology, 15*(2), 315-331.

Viswanatian, M. (1997). Individual Differences in Need for Precision. *Personality and Social Psychology Bulletin, 23*(7), 717-735.

Webster, D. M., & Kruglanski, A. W. (1994). Individual differences in need for cognitive closure. *Journal of Personality and Social Psychology, 67*(6), 1049-1062.

White, C. M., & Hoffrage, U. (2009). Testing the Tyranny of Too Much Choice Against the Allure of More Choice. *Psychology, 26,* 280-298.

INDEX

According to my Ph.D. supervisor, and one of the smartest people I have met, Prof. Emile Aarts, a book without an Index is not a book. So here is the Index: